Area Map

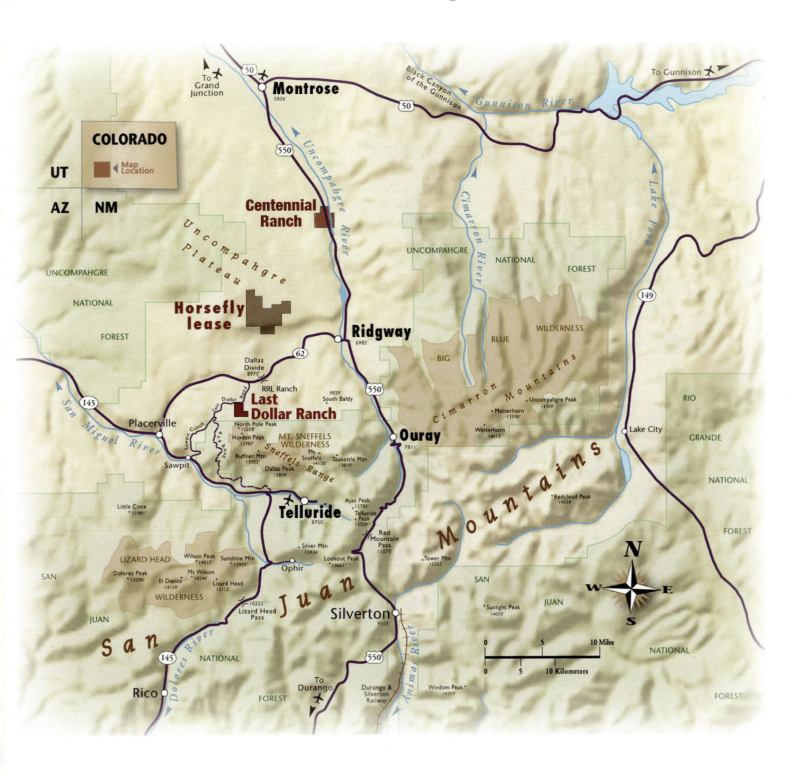

The Life and Times of Vince Kontny

VOLUME 4: THE GOLDEN YEARS

"I had rather be on my farm than be emperor of the world."
— George Washington

Vince Kontny   First Edition 2016

Cover photo by Chris Marona: Jason on the lines while I kick off flakes.

Double Shoe Publishing Company
35000 South Highway 550
Montrose, Colorado 81403

Printed in Canada

Copyright © 2016
All rights reserved
Vince Kontny

ISBN-10: 0975881264
ISBN-13: 978-0-9758812-6-2
Four-Volume Set ISBN-10: 0975881272
Four-Volume Set ISBN-13: 978-0-9758812-7-9

PCN: 2010932198

Author:	**Editor:**	**Designer:**
Vince Kontny	Jeri Mattics	Jody Mattics
Centennial Ranch	62768 North Star Drive	66140 Crestview Dr.
35000 South Highway 550	Montrose, CO 81403	Montrose, CO 81403
Montrose, CO 81403	Phone: 970-209-4511	Phone: 970-275-0034
Phone: 970-240-3822	E-mail: jmo@rmmc.biz	E-mail: jmattics@me.com
E-mail: vincekontny@gmail.com		

Acknowledgments

If not for these four ladies, this book would never have seen the light of day. I'm extremely grateful.

Barbara Parker

We have been a close team for longer than Barbara probably wants to admit. Initially, she was an executive assistant during our corporate years. Then, Barbara retired and moved to Colorado to look after all things administrative on our ranches.

After 10 years, Barbara moved to New York and eventually Arizona to be near her family. She accepted the daunting task of deciphering my handwriting for all of my *Life and Times* books. One couldn't have a more professional, loyal or dedicated friend.

Jody Mattics

Jody is a gifted graphic designer with an admirable work ethic and a delicious sense of humor. The quality of her layout work on all my volumes has received numerous compliments from national book award judges as well as an untold number of readers. She has been a joy to work with due to her patience and ability, always with a smile, to accommodate requests and changes.

Natalie Heller

For this volume, which covers my family's experience with Colorado ranching, much of the story can be better told with images than text. Natalie's intense interest, ability with her trusty Canon, and her willingness to brave the elements, fast-approaching large animals, hot branding irons and temperamental cowboys to capture what ranching can still be like in the fading West has been an integral part of preserving our history for publication. You will be as thankful, as I am, when you see her contributions in the later chapters of this book. Natalie often gives credit to the axiom, "A picture is worth a thousand words."

Jeri Mattics

Jeri is a person with a broad spectrum of extraordinary talents for all manner of communication. She is continually providing wise, educated counsel to me, an engineer who writes but admittedly is not a writer. In addition, Jeri manages all phases of the writing and publishing process. Acting in this capacity, she contributed her judgment and experience to all my books while also working as the editor.

Contents

Acknowledgements i

Contents ii

Dedications- Duane Beamer iv

      Ted Moews vi

   Jason Middleton vii

Im Memoriam - Joan Kontny x

      Garret Middleton xi

Editor's Note xii

Foreword xiv

Introduction xvi

Chapter One: Returning to My Roots. Why? 1

Chapter Two: My Quest: A Working Cattle Ranch in the
San Juan Mountains of Southwest Colorado 9

Chapter Three: Finding the Last Dollar 13

Chapter Four: A Brief History of Last Dollar 17

Chapter Five: Saving Last Dollar 28

Chapter Six: Protection of Last Dollar in Perpetuity- 61
   As Long as the Grass Grows and the Rivers Flow

Chapter Seven: A Day in the Life of Last Dollar, circa 1935 65

Chapter Eight: The Sister Ranch - Centennial 81

Chapter Nine: A Brief History of Centennial..89

Chapter Ten: Saving Centennial 103

Chapter Eleven: Protection of Centennial in Perpetuity -..................... 140
    As Long as the Grass Grows and the Rivers Flow

Chapter Twelve: A Day in the Life of Centennial, circa 1935............................ 143

Chapter Thirteen: Ranch Life 151

- The Beef Business
- Brands
- Our Brand
- Our Cattle Company
- Ranch Families
- Weddings

- Cowboys
- Cowboy Gear
- Horse Gear
- Ranch Animals
  - Horses
  - Dogs
  - Wildlife
  - Cattle

- Annual Ranch Activities
  - Winter Feeding
  - Calving
  - Branding
  - Breeding
  - Haying
  - High Country
  - Gather
  - Cattle Drive
  - Calf Sales

Chapter Fourteen: Commercial Photo Shoots....................................201

- Last Dollar Ranch
- Centennial Ranch

Chapter Fifteen: Kids at the Ranch 225

Chapter Sixteen: Double Shoe Publishing Company...........................240

- *Smith Ranch*, Colona, Colorado, 1879-1992

- *Last Dollar Ranch* - 1993, *Last Dollar Ranch,* Second Edition - 2005

- *Heritage in Iron* - 2004

- *A Ranching Legacy* - 2005

- *The Life & Times of Vince Kontny*
  - Volume 1: The Early Years - 2010
  - Volume 2: The Seabees & Me - 2011
  - Volume 3: A Career in Construction - 2013
  - Volume 4: The Golden Years - 2016

Dedication

Duane Beamer

If you, the reader, do not know Duane Beamer personally, you soon will if you continue to thumb through the book in your hands. I am fortunate in that he was not only my respected partner in the quest to acquire, restore and protect two historic ranches in Colorado and then to operate them as working cattle ranches in the manner of their long heritage, but also he is a dear friend with a great sense of humor.

I first met Duane when I began to realize the dream of returning to my agricultural roots. Since that day, Duane has been invaluable in making that dream a decades-long reality. He is a man of many skills, those of true cowboy traits with horses, cattle, dogs, wildlife, et al. He is also a gifted manager as a builder with rare carpentry skills and a working knowledge of many other crafts.

Regarding Duane, an anonymous friend wrote the following in our first book, *Last Dollar Ranch*: "What really sets Duane apart is not his many capabilities, but his character. He has honesty,

integrity and a willingness to do whatever it takes combined with a sincere love for the land, the animals and the ranching way of life. Duane would never ask a man to do a job he wouldn't do himself, and he wouldn't hesitate to help out a neighbor no matter what the task, the time or the temperature. His approach to life is like that of the pioneers who originally settled Hastings Mesa—he works the land with his own hands and a lot of heart." This friend continued: "He is a genuine renaissance man of the West." I can't beat that description.

The good news today is that Duane has passed all these attributes on to his family—his wonderful wife, Amy, and two children, Jenna and Hasten, of whom he can be very proud.

Country

FOR THOSE WHO LIVE IN OR LONG FOR THE COUNTRY

JUNE/JULY/98
$2.99 U.S./$3.99 CANADA

Chris Marona

Chris Marona

Chris Marona

Dedication

Ted Moews

Within days of buying the Last Dollar Ranch and following an early heavy snowfall, I met Ted Moews (pronounced Maze). The snow on the roof of the large log cow barn was pushing the walls out. With more snow, it would surely have collapsed.

I desperately asked for some advice from the seller, Bob Corey. He said he knew the man that could save the nearly century-old barn. Within hours, Ted was there. Working in the loft, we installed strands of heavy wire from wall to wall then twisted them taut. It saved the barn. Since that first meeting, Ted has been invaluable in the restoration of old structures and the design and construction of new ones on both ranches. His thumbprints are everywhere.

From his earliest years living on the wild edge of our state (he helped build his first log cabin when he was 12 years old), Ted has contributed enormously to the preservation and appreciation of the Old West. Fast forward to the present. Ted and Katie, his wife, live off the grid in a cabin at an elevation of 10,000 feet, built nearly four decades ago just a mile above the Last Dollar homestead. He felled the timber for their cabin from their small acreage and skidded the logs out with a team of horses.

Ted's artistic talents were developed while pursuing fine arts degrees from the University of Denver and UCLA. Later, while still in California, Ted taught a diversity of art forms including pottery, stained glass, pencil sketching and bronze sculpting in addition to water color and oil painting.

Over time, Ted was drawn back to his first love, Colorado. In the Centennial state, he found an outlet for his artistic design capabilities in the construction of log cabins and barns, and his design of functional iron by working with some of the country's leading blacksmiths.

It is for his numerous contributions to our ranches that this book is respectfully dedicated.

Dedication

Jason Middleton

Jason joined the Double Shoe Cattle Company a decade ago as the manager of Centennial Ranch. He is an extraordinary individual who has made an invaluable contribution to the daily and seasonal workings of the ranch.

Arriving as a young man with his wife, Corin, and their two children, Chelsea and Garret, Jason brought experience, skills and a work ethic developed by a background in local ranching. Jason is a true horseman with a keen eye for spotting cows in trouble; he has the innate ability to doctor them back to good health. Jason is a farrier, spur maker, welder and mechanic and keeps everything running smoothly.

On winter mornings, Jason, another ranch hand, Benito Fernandez, and I would harness the Belgians, load the hay wagon by hand with small bales, then feed the hungry cows (as shown on the cover of this book). To share in that chore has been the highlight of my own ranch memories. When Benito left to assume a position on a large spread to the east, Jason managed the ranch single-handedly. Centennial Ranch today stands as a tribute to his dedication.

He is, as they say in the West, "a damned good man," not only as a manager but also as a husband and father. I will always be indebted to Jason for his dedication and deep appreciation for the ways of the Old West.

Chris Marona

Natalie Heller

Natalie Heller

Natalie Heller

In Memoriam

Joan Dashwood Kontny

28 October 1943 - 7 December 2013

To live on in the hearts we leave behind...

In Memoriam

Garret Carl Middleton

6 February 1999 - 19 April 2014

Garret arrived at Centennial with his family—Dad Jason, Mom Corin and sister Chelsea—when he was just five years old. A decade later we lost him in a tragic accident. He was immensely popular with our young grandchildren when they visited the ranch as he was always available, patient and fun. Garret was truly a fine young man. We miss him.

Branding 2014

is not to die.

Editor's Note:

Ted Moews is a bit of a paradox: rough and tough on the outside, sophisticated and smooth as silk when you take a moment to get to know him a little better. Physically, Ted is a grizzly bear of a guy. Not only does he frequently dress like a mountain man, at 6' 5" he is a mountain of a man. Those who "judge this book by its cover" likely admire Ted's dedication to living a simple life, but probably never realize his enormous talents as an artist and educator.

A natural, gifted artist, Ted has an extraordinary sense of space, texture, color and mass that is evident in all that he designs and builds. Ted's artistic talents were developed while earning a Bachelor of Fine Arts degree from the University of Denver (in drawing and fine arts) and a Master of Fine Arts Degree from UCLA (in sculpture). After graduating, Ted taught pottery, stained glass, pencil sketching and bronze sculpting in addition to watercolor and oil painting in the University of California system. He worked with students ranging from those in the elementary grades to graduate students in art.

Ted chuckles when remembering how his relationship with Vince developed. "Katie and I had snowmobiled past the Last Dollar buildings for years, watching them slowly fall apart in this harsh climate," he said. "I first met Vince with Duane and discovered we shared a number of common interests."

"At first, to Vince, I was just a laborer, helping to save the cow barn. When we were restoring the hog shed, I suggested we should raise it up and place a stone wall under it. Vince wondered aloud what that would look like and I offered to draw him a picture," Ted chuckled. As you might imagine, his drawing of how he envisioned restoring the hog barn wasn't exactly the sketch of a novice.

Even though Ted had grown up ranching and rodeoing, it turned out that Vince had hired an accomplished artist, log builder/architect and western historian who has had numerous articles by and about his work in such diverse magazines as *Architectural Digest, Western Horseman, New Pioneer, Log Home Building, Cowboys & Indians, Southwest Art* and many others.

Ted has restored old historic forts and created ranch buildings for a number of notables, Ralph Lauren among them. In addition, his work has won recognition both here and abroad. The editors of *New Pioneer* magazine said "Ted Moews is arguably the leading designer of log homes in the country today".

Over time, Ted has done everything from help Vince save the original log buildings on the Last Dollar Ranch from a century of winter's heavy snow loads to designing many of the structures and the intricate custom-made wrought iron hardware pieces that adorn the Last Dollar and Centennial Ranches.

Through the years and this wide variety of projects, Ted and Vince had the opportunity to work together, share philosophies and trade stories. Having both "escaped" southern California and selected Hastings Mesa as their landing spot, Ted and Vince found they had much in common. They developed a deep appreciation for each other's skill sets and overall approach to life and its challenges. As such, Ted has an interesting perspective to share about this book's author.

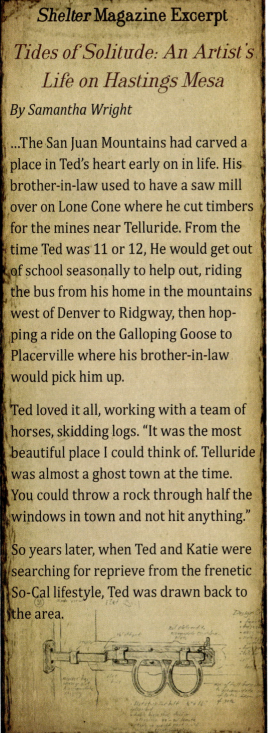

Shelter Magazine Excerpt

Tides of Solitude: An Artist's Life on Hastings Mesa

By Samantha Wright

...The San Juan Mountains had carved a place in Ted's heart early on in life. His brother-in-law used to have a saw mill over on Lone Cone where he cut timbers for the mines near Telluride. From the time Ted was 11 or 12, He would get out of school seasonally to help out, riding the bus from his home in the mountains west of Denver to Ridgway, then hopping a ride on the Galloping Goose to Placerville where his brother-in-law would pick him up.

Ted loved it all, working with a team of horses, skidding logs. "It was the most beautiful place I could think of. Telluride was almost a ghost town at the time. You could throw a rock through half the windows in town and not hit anything."

So years later, when Ted and Katie were searching for reprieve from the frenetic So-Cal lifestyle, Ted was drawn back to the area.

Foreword

By Ted Moews

Imagine what it would be like if we could peek into the myriads of lives around us. If we could pick and choose and then touch (if only briefly) their "stories" in passing…

Looking through that lens we have been allowed glimpses into the life of Vince Kontny, one of the truly interesting men of the 20th century whose story was forged from an amalgam of unique parts.

Early life on the endless Great Plains under the big sky imbued a humbling feeling for the vast sweep of God's creation and his place in it. War creates awareness of another kind of humbling experience: mortality. Kontny's time in Vietnam showed him the importance of working together, of leadership, of delegating and of recognizing the invaluable (sometimes lifesaving) bond that men form in times of danger.

Sifting these elements through the screen of his leadership years in international enterprise riveted together the man we see in this later chapter of his life. A man who has learned the value of seeking out, understanding, appreciating and openly acknowledging the unique value diverse individuals can bring through teamwork.

Vince dealt with the pressures associated with his leadership role in international companies by harboring plans for someday buying and building a ranch. In times of stress, or perhaps just when the burdens of life seemed particularly heavy, he would sit back in his chair at the office or on a long international flight to somewhere and escape to his "ranch."

Just so we don't get too serious, I have to interject here and paraphrase one of Vince's favorite pieces of advice from his father: "Son, if you really want a cattle ranch, get a good job first so you can afford it." (Vince's humorous sense of perspective runs like a thread through all he does.)

His life stream led him to fulfill that private goal: a working "ranch" somewhere in God's country (the high Rocky Mountains of Colorado) where:

- he could create a lifestyle and a legacy for his family

- his children could experience some of the values inherent in that kind of a ranching environment

Where else can you glimpse such a microcosm of this world, it's joys and sorrows? The birth of new life, the finality of death, the deep friendship and cooperation among neighboring ranching families. Where your word  and a firm handshake are your bond. Having your children learn that taking care of their animals and their chores comes before personal gratification. Living close to the land and in tune with the seasons gives children a deeper understanding and strength that can carry them all the days of their lives.

Vince is, above all, a visionary who loves to build and create. Who else would find an abandoned falling-down ranch in one of the most spectacular locations in the Rocky Mountain West and see through the piles of rotted timber, tumbledown fences and lost dreams to a future where that historical legacy could live again? Most people would bulldoze the place and start afresh. He alone saw the potential and restored as well as enhanced what to most would have been a lost cause.

This is that story... Take a deep breath, find a comfortable seat and savor every page.

Introduction

Born and raised the ninth of 10 children on the Great Plains of Northeast Colorado where the country is so flat you can watch your dog run away for three days, there was no doubt during those early years that I would be a cattleman someday.

When I was about 10 years old, my parents introduced the younger members of our family to the wonders of the Colorado mountains. The dark blue skies, majestic mountains, meadows full of beautiful wild flowers, and clear streams with brook trout seemingly winking at me changed my life's ambition. Being a cattleman was still the goal, but with this new exposure to God's work in Colorado, I wanted to spend most of my life on a working cattle ranch in the mountains rather than on the plains.

My father poured a little cold water on this ambition. He said it simply wasn't possible to make enough money ranching to support a family. His advice: get an education, work hard at a real job, educate your children, then and only then—if you still want a mountain ranch—buy one and move in. It was good advice, and I took it.

After graduating from college there was little doubt I would serve in the military; my father was president of the local draft board. Instead of waiting to be drafted into the Army for two years, I volunteered for the Navy Seabees planning to serve for four years. As an officer, it was a unique experience during an interesting time.

I spent my enlistment (and the additional two years I extended) in the Pacific and Southeast Asia during the early years of the Vietnam War. Much of my time with the Seabees was spent on independent duty with its broad responsibilities.

Upset with the public treatment of returning servicemen from Vietnam, I elected not to return to the United States. Receiving my discharge in Bangkok, I caught the next train to Singapore and from there, a flight to Australia.

> "Twenty-nine years after I started work on the Outback railway, I retired from that company as president. It was the largest engineering/construction company in the world at the time with some 30,000 employees and an equal number of subcontractors with operations in 67 countries. I worked on all seven continents. However, the dream of a working cattle ranch in the mountains of Colorado had never faded."

It was tough finding a job there, but I finally landed one as a laborer on an Outback railway project with a large American engineering/construction company. Despite the humble beginnings, it was to become the good job my father had recommended.

Twenty-nine years after I started work on the Outback railway, I retired from that company as president. It was the largest engineering/construction company in the world at the time with some 30,000 employees and an equal number of subcontractors with operations in 67 countries. I worked on all seven continents. However, the dream of a working cattle ranch in the mountains of Colorado had never faded.

With our three children educated and off on their own journeys through life, my wife, Joan, and I started our search for a small mountain ranch where we could live the good life, raise a few cattle, and hopefully protect the ranch and lifestyle for future generations.

Our focus was in beautiful, unspoiled southwest Colorado. In 1989, we bought the 400-acre historic and drop-dead gorgeous Last Dollar Ranch near Ridgway. Three years later, we added another small ranch, Centennial. It also had a proud past and, in addition, was a full half-mile lower in elevation so it could produce winter feed and provide a good environment for calving in the spring. Both ranches were protected from any development in perpetuity with donated conservation easements.

Once we had acquired these two ranches with their rich, century-long histories, we created our own publishing company. The intent was to capture the history of the two ranches before the players passed on. Two hardcover books were produced.

In 2003, Joan and I moved our permanent residence to Dashwood House on Centennial Ranch. Once settled, we published two additional books, *A Heritage in Iron*, to pay tribute to the skilled artists and blacksmiths who created the functional ironwork on both ranches, and *A Ranching Legacy*, with amazing photography and artwork describing the ranches and the cattle operations. Each of these books received three national book awards.

At the urging of my three children to document my interesting life experiences for their children and future grandchildren, I set about the task of writing four volumes entitled *The Life and Times of Vince Kontny*. *Volume 1: The Early Years* chronicles my life on the Great Plains and through college. The next installment, *Volume 2: The Seabees and Me*, covers my six years as a Naval officer with the Seabees in the Pacific and Southeast Asia. My long career in international engineering and construction is the subject of *Volume 3: A Career in Construction*. Finally, the book you are holding in your hands, *Volume 4: The Golden Years*, covers the time and activities of my life as a rancher in Southwest Colorado.

This book attempts to give the reader a feel for the place, people and history of our two ranches, and the western lifestyle along with the effort to preserve them for future generations. There are no more books contemplated. My future is, of course, uncertain. It has been a richly rewarding and enjoyable life and a great hour to live. In this part of my life I will paraphrase Jameson Parker with an excerpt from his book *An Accidental Cowboy*. "I was OK on a horse, but would never claim to be a real cowboy. I'm not smart enough, knowledgable enough, or tough enough. But I did have fun!"

Now there is really only one certainty—I will never sell my saddle.

Enjoy!
Vince

Returning To My Agricultural Roots

Why?

For readers of my first volume, *The Life and Times of Vince Kontny: The Early Years,* you will be familiar with my experiences of being born and raised on a Western Great Plains farm and ranch. The ninth of ten children, it was one of my life's most enjoyable and developmental periods.

Larry (aka Vince), Rod and Jim, 1941

My parents' last three children were all boys—my brother Jim, two years older, myself, and my brother, Rod, some three years younger. I was known as "Larry" until I joined the Navy.

Rod was just a little squirt during those years on the ranch, so he didn't participate much in our early adventures. However, Jim and I were close in age and development. We spent all day every day in a constant search of fun and mischief. As I noted only half facetiously, except during blizzards and dust storms, we were turned loose after breakfast with the unstated but well understood direction that we should not return to the house until dinner (lunch in today's vocabulary) unless we were bleeding or on fire.

It was a good life with exposure to the complete spectrum of farm animals common at the time. We could do whatever our imaginations might present—like trying to sneak into a pig pen to hold a piglet while the sow dozed. But, one sudden squeal and we had just a single second of time to drop the cute little pig and clear the fence for safety beyond. In the clear vision of hindsight, a failed attempt at that fence may well have ended what turned out to be a long life.

Jim and me in our Sunday best

Without close supervision, or, in reality, no supervision because the men were occupied with constant chores and the women were busy with endless household and kitchen tasks, Jim and I were free to roam. It was only during our days at our one-room school (seven total students—three of which were Kontnys) that our elders were relieved of the concerns regarding what we were up to that day.

When I was but five years old, I would carry a bolt-action .410 shotgun, along with Jim similarly armed with his single-shot 20-gauge. We would walk the fields for hours in pursuit of anything larger than a mouse. Jackrabbits were the prey of choice, but we seldom ever actually pulled the trigger since we had only a couple shells each with no reliable means of resupply. If three jackrabbits were in line, it was okay to shoot—just two, probably not.

If times became really boring, we could always, and frequently, retreat to the hulk of a Model-A Ford deep in the orchard to have a satisfying cigarette we had pinched from our older brother's top dresser drawer. There were no health warnings on the pack of Camels in those days, and even if there were, we couldn't read anyway. But, I'm glad it wasn't a habit that persisted. I have famously, and accurately, stated that I quit smoking at six when we moved to town.

Neither my Dad nor my older brothers were ever to be confused with real cowboys, although we had a couple of saddle horses, which were augmented with a gentle team of draft horses for field work. With so many kids, I believe Dad was somewhat pressured by family and neighbors to get Jim and me a pony. That pony could have killed both me and my later burning desire to be a cattleman. With an IQ that exceeded that of both Jim and myself combined, that pony called our bluff every time and never gave us anything but grief.

Jim and me on our rough-stock bucking bronc.

An older brother would saddle it, pitch one or both of us on top, then hand us the reins. We kicked his sides as hard as we could to no avail. After a few minutes, someone would find a stick and give the pony a good whack on the rump. The critter would jump in an attempt to induce a serious backlash injury, then trot four steps (enough to clear the stick's range) before decelerating to a slow walk. It knew perfectly well what to do next–head for the trees. Mind you, it was seeking a particular tree that it knew well. The tree had a low, horizontal branch, just high enough to clear the saddle horn, but low enough to relieve him of the annoying burden on his back.

Jim and I would pull furiously on the reins, both initially then just one at a time. The pony was unfazed and soon we could see the low branch approaching.

> It was indeed a good life, but during those early years on the farm with Jim, there were valuable lessons to be learned that would form the foundation of my work ethic and the principles that guided me through my entire life. During this time on the ranch, our heroes—those we looked up to and wanted to emulate—were those men (and women) we observed daily.

As always, at the last second we would grab the branch while the pony continued on its path. Suspended in mid-air, we would then drop to the ground where we could relieve our frustration by violently kicking a few rocks.

It was indeed a good life, but during those early years on the farm with Jim, there were valuable lessons to be learned that would form the foundation of my work ethic and the principles that guided me through my entire life. During this time on the ranch, our heroes—those we looked up to and wanted to emulate—were those men (and women) we observed daily. This was an age before mass communication. Our only exposure was the ½-hour program we listened to religiously every Saturday morning—the Buster Brown adventure story series introduced in 1943. There we were huddled on the floor of the dining room in front of our upright radio with its scratchy speakers in a trance listening to that week's adventure. Sound effects were so realistic one would shudder with chills as the cowboy on a horse pushed some half-frozen cows toward the barn during a blizzard, and this was on a hot day in July!

Today kids seem possessed with idols they never meet, whether they be rock stars or football standouts. Look at the posters tacked on the wall of a teenager's bedroom and you can appreciate what I'm saying.

We indeed had our heroes—those that lived and worked on the farm. Hard-working and tough, our heroes had great attitudes and senses of humor and being. Those were the people we wanted to be like when we grew up. Our heroes were guided by their own code, which we would respect and which would form our own moral foundation for the rest of our lives.

The Code of the West

During the early days of the Old West, and in this context I'm referring to the time of the "Open Range" that existed after the Civil War until the earliest barbed wire fences were built about 1880, there were few laws and fewer lawmen. There was an unwritten code of behavior for those working cowboys that would become legends and icons in our nation's history. They were guided by what is known as the Cowboy's Code. Here are a few self-explanatory examples of this code:

• Never steal another man's horse.

• Always help someone in need—even a stranger.

• Your work is your bond.

• A firm handshake is more binding than a written contract.

• Be there for a friend in need.

• Cuss all you want—but never around women.

The list goes on, but you get the picture.

Over the early years, this Cowboy Code morphed into what has become known as the Code of the West—again, unwritten until 1934 when Zane Grey wrote his novel, *the Code of the West*. Since then, more have tried to define this broader code, more of principles than simply behavior. The Code is timeless, as applicable today in society and business as in the early days. An excellent illustration is the book *Cowboy Ethics—What Wall Street Can Learn from the Code of the West* by James P. Owen.

My father, who had to quit school after the third grade to work full time on a farm to support himself and his family, was the very embodiment of the Code of the West. He lived every day by the code and the principles it encompassed. He never lectured me on these principles, but rather taught me by his actions I observed. He was my hero and the guiding light during my life.

A few lessons from simpler times
Character, Principles and Values

- When you take on a task do it well, and take pride in your work. No matter how seemingly insignificant a chore might be, give it your best shot.

  > I am concerned with what I perceive as a poor work ethic in much of the younger generation.

- Don't quit. Always finish what you start, whether it be a job, raising kids, whatever.

  > Dad never quit, and reaped the rewards of a super strong work ethic, moral character and dedication.

- Practice the Golden Rule every day.

  > When we moved to the small town of Julesburg, Colorado, we lived in a house just a couple of blocks from the railroad tracks. In those days there was a fair amount of hobo traffic still riding the rails, and they seemed to pass the word that there would be a meal for the asking at the Kontnys, where Mom would prepare a huge Dagwood sandwich for them served with fresh fruit. Mother's last words to each was to repay her actions with their own hospitality to someone less fortunate once they got on their feet again.

- Ride for the brand

  > This is a holdover code from the earliest cowboy's code when it was expected that hired hands be loyal to their ranch, regardless of the hardships, weather or the task. The only exception to this rule was if the employer was doing something unethical. Then, if one couldn't influence a change in the practice, the cowboy should simply quit, as a matter of principle, and move on.

- One's word or a firm handshake should be as good, or better, than a written contract.

From humble beginnings with his young family on a rented farm, my father eventually accumulated several thousand acres of prime farmland. As a silent observer on several of these land transactions, in the absence of either lawyers or real estate agents, the terms were agreed and the deal was sealed with a handshake. When the transaction was made over the phone, his word was all that was required. To the best of my knowledge, he was never sued.

This is a trait I valued during my entire working career. Joan and I purchased the Centennial Ranch in 1992 from the three Smith Brothers, whose family had owned the ranch for over a century and had sold their calves for several years to my dad some 400 miles away, sight unseen. I sat in their ranch house drinking coffee and agreed on the terms. It was sealed when I stood up and extended my hand to each of the brothers—the deal was done. The paperwork would follow. There was never a problem.

There are other principles in the Code of the West, *all still applicable in today's modern world.*

My Early Thoughts for a Career

During my years in primary education and later in high school, my single life's ambition was to be a cattleman like my father. After we moved from our ranch into the small, rural town of Julesburg in Colorado, just a mile from the Nebraska border, my father built a feedlot where he would buy quality calves weighing about 600 pounds and finish them with a high grain diet to some 1,200 pounds of excellent beef animals grading USDA "choice" and some "prime."

Every chance available to me was spent with Dad at that feedlot—feeding, doctoring and sorting cattle for the market. From my earliest days at the ranch, I was exposed to men who worked hard and lived by the *Code of the West*. I wanted to emulate my father and those men whom I highly respected; but it was during this period that I added another vision for my future ranching life. That new dimension was an introduction to the magnificent mountains of Colorado.

The Unsurpassed Glory of the Mountains

Living on the Western Great Plains where it was said that the land was so flat you could watch your dog run away for three days, Jim and I were totally ignorant of what wonders existed in Western Colorado. Our first introduction to the mountains came when our parents organized a week-long summer vacation for us "three little boys" to the mountains as our first-ever family vacation.

They arranged to rent a small rustic cabin in the woods next to a beautiful little creek with crystal clear water—home to some brook trout. What an eye opener! And what fun! Our horizons had been indelibly expanded —literally. With our newly discovered playground expanded, all we asked for was more. Never ending chores at the ranch precluded our parents from satisfying our constant pleas for trips to the mountains, so they farmed Jim and me out each summer for two weeks to attend Camp St. Malo near Estes Park in the heart of the beautiful Rocky Mountains.

It was a wonderful Catholic camp for mostly inner-city boys with the full spectrum of well-organized daily activities followed by mass in the evening at a beautiful little church, Chapel on the Rock. Pope John Paul II visited the chapel during his trip to the U.S. in 1993 for World Youth Day.

Chapel on the Rock

It was more than just a great time at the camp. After several summers of camp, our sister, Betty, then a teacher in Denver, arranged for her mountain-obsessed friends, Dave and Gudy Gaskill, to give us a two-week intensive introduction to the wonders of Colorado's mountainous world.

For two weeks we camped (every night), fished, hiked, climbed two "fourteeners" and received constant tutoring in the pleasures and preservation of this unspoiled wilderness.

Enjoying the view

The top of a "Fourteener"

Setting up camp

Primitive rafting

At the end of that life-changing two weeks, my ranching ambitions had been expanded— it was now a working cattle ranch in the high mountains. I even developed an image in my mind of what that ranch would look like, an image that never changed until it was realized many decades later.

I described this image in the Foreword of the book, *A Ranching Legacy*, I published after acquiring our mountain ranches.

> "While still in high school, I had a dream, literally, of this ranch. While some of the details of this dream are fuzzy, one image has remained with me. There is a stream on the left, always on the left, with crystal-clear water rushing over rocks in a setting of aspen and blue spruce. The stream, which one can walk across, is full of pan-sized trout. In the background are majestic mountains rising to the clouds. Contented Hereford cows and calves graze in the meadows and horses stand in the corrals next to a large log-and-stone barn. That visual has been indelibly printed in my brain. It has never changed."

My father became aware of this new ambition. He was then, and continues to this day, to be the greatest influence in my life. Dad's strong work ethic, dedication to his family and church, being tough but fair, honest almost to a fault, his word and handshake sealed even the largest transaction—a true patriot and one who lived by the principles of the *Code of the West*.

The lessons of my father were almost exclusively by observation while we ate and worked as opposed to verbal recitations, so it came as a bit of a surprise that he told me what I should do before pursuing my dream of a working cattle ranch in the mountains. Again, I quote from my Foreword:

> "My goal in life was established—I wanted a ranch in the mountains. However, my father gave me some good advice. He said ranching was simply not that profitable, and that I should get an education, then a good job to support and educate my family. Once that was accomplished, I could get a little ranch in the mountains. It was good counsel, and I took it."

Following college, my dream of a mountain ranch never faded as I volunteered to serve in the U.S. Navy with the Seabees in Southwest Asia (*Volume 2: The Seabees and Me*) and later, during a long career in the international engineering/construction industry (*Volume 3: A Career in Construction*).

My dream of having a ranch has never wavered and as I write this chapter, it has been realized. Perhaps you, the reader, will still wonder about the "Why" in the chapter heading, but living on the Centennial Ranch with a strong river flowing within a few feet of my desk, working with outstanding men (see the Dedication), and with family, friends and neighbors that adhere to the principles of the Code of the West, I believe you can understand the "why."

My Quest: A Working Cattle Ranch in the Colorado Mountains

Having locked in on this ranching dream at an early age, it would be decades before it would be affordable and eventually realized. But, the desire and vision would never fade.

Eventually, I would marry my Aussie bride, Joan, and the union would soon produce three beautiful children: Natascha, Michael and Amber. When they were old enough to stand upright on skies, we started what would become a family tradition, celebrating a white Christmas at a ski resort in the Western Untied States. During that period my job with Fluor Corporation kept us either in Australia or sunny Southern California, so a vacation in the snow was a real treat for everyone and we all enjoyed them immensely.

Christmas destinations took us to Mammoth, California; Sun Valley, Idaho; Taos, New Mexico; and finally to Aspen, Colorado. For the next several years we continued to return to Aspen. We rented a comfortable, modestly priced condo convenient to all the downtown shops and restaurants as well as the shuttle bus to the slopes. It was always a grand time in Aspen with the geographic advantage of allowing us to visit my parents in northeast Colorado near the end of our vacation.

By the time we started coming to Aspen, I would always carve out a few hours to take the family out into the surrounding countryside to see the creeks, meadows and mountains and to begin the sales pitch of how wonderful it would be if we could ever live in such a place. It was an easy sale.

When the kids were in middle and high school, I suggested we go to a new resort, Telluride, in southwest Colorado. An old mining town in a gorgeous hanging valley, it had tons of character with the complete spectrum of easy-to-challenging ski runs and a wide assortment of good, fun restaurants. Michael, at that time, had a cast on his foot from a football injury, so I cut off the 18" tip from an old ski and fashioned him a long thong binding to wrap around the moon boot over his cast. So, he had a long ski on one foot and a short ski on the other. He never even slowed down, but soon switched to a snowboard.

Again, we took a few trips out of Telluride to check out the surrounding area. It was wonderful. The San Juan Mountains are the youngest in the Rocky Mountains and therefore the most rugged. They also contain many of the state's highest peaks. There were other advantages, for us at least, in this corner of Colorado. It was remote from the state's population to the east. Being remote (a 6-to-7-hour drive from Denver over good roads) the real estate market, particularly for ranches and open space, was a bargain compared to prices being asked near other ski resorts in the state.

This was indeed the area to realize my dream of having a mountain ranch. But with an individual minded independent family, I had to carefully—very carefully—sell the idea to those involved. I was working on the premise that each member of the family had a vote (four votes for Joan and the kids), but what I failed to mention was that I had five votes, and being a democracy, the majority of votes would prevail. Really, I needed a unanimous endorsement.

For me, this area was definitely the place. But it wasn't time to spring the idea on the family. So while still in Telluride, I suggested we return for a week in the summer to see if the warm activities were as good as the cold. Everyone was enthusiastic with that idea.

So, about the first of July in 1989, we arrived by car to spend a week at the San Juan Guest Ranch just 45 minutes from Telluride between the small rural towns of Ouray and Ridgway.

It was a great week riding good horses, fishing, camping, hiking and sightseeing.

On the Fourth of July, it was the ranch's tradition to view a spectacular fireworks display in the mountain amphitheater just above Ouray, a small mountain town known as the Switzerland of America.

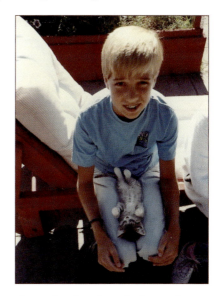

The cook at the ranch packed a delicious picnic dinner for all the guests and those that worked at the ranch as well as a few select friends who helped with the horses and guided the fall hunting trips. In ranch transportation, the guests arrived at a reserved little high meadow well before sunset. We enjoyed the picnic, but soon our ample supply of beer was exhausted. I offered to buy a couple of cases in Ouray but I needed transport. That is how I first met Duane Beamer who would become my ranching partner and good friend for decades and to whom this book is dedicated.

Duane was invited to the picnic because he was a good friend of the guest ranch manager, Scott McTiernan. Duane and his father, Russ, were both excellent farriers and once a month would come on a weekend during the only vacant day between guest arrivals/departures to put new shoes on all the horses.

I had noticed Duane at the picnic, he was a true cowboy: slim, wearing a black hat, chambray shirt, jeans and boots. He was authentic, his hat had been long introduced to both sweat and dust and with his trimmed bushy mustache he was strikingly handsome. There was one gesture of his I observed that qualified him as a gentleman.

When introduced to a female guest he had not previously met, he extended his right hand for a gentle handshake while his left hand instinctively rose to his hat brim for a slight tip. I was impressed by that *Code of the West* courtesy, which is a habit he exhibits even to the present day. Duane would also act as a hunting guide for Scott's guests during the fall deer and elk hunts.

Duane introduced himself as the driver for our beer run and guided me to his nearly antique, faded green flatbed pickup. I quietly thought we could make it to town okay, but I wasn't as confident that we could make it back up the hill.

> After a couple hours of private conversation to work out some details and to solidify our personal visions, we sealed the deal in the tradition of the *Code of the West*—
> with a firm handshake.

My years in the construction field had enabled me to develop a valuable talent: to quickly, and generally accurately, evaluate a man's character and skills without them realizing it. So with Duane I asked a cascade of friendly, innocent questions on his background, work experience, and most importantly, clues to his character. He was raised by his genuine cowboy father and mother on a ranch in eastern Colorado and was exposed to all the cowboy skills at a very early age. He even took up leatherwork in 4-H, making a nicely tooled purse for his mother and a belt for his no-nonsense father.

He finished high school with a well-earned tough reputation as a wrestler, while continuing to work on local cattle ranches. After high school, he got a job with a man building high-end quality homes in northern Colorado. It was with the patience and dedication of this man that Duane learned the intricate skills of a finish carpenter.

After less than 30 minutes of our beer run, I was more than just satisfied that I had found the man to partner with to realize my ranching ambition. He was young and fit with the full spectrum of skills needed for a ranch manger: good horseman; farrier; experienced with cattle—from calving, and branding to doctoring; and a good cabinet maker—experienced with building and contracting. Perhaps most of all, he was intelligent, honest with high moral values and a delicious sense of humor.

We agreed to meet the next day to outline our separate ambitions. He would find a suitable ranch, help me acquire it, then manage the restoration and eventual cattle operations. In doing so, he would make my dream come true as well as his to manage a working cattle ranch.

After a couple hours of private conversation to work out some details and to solidify our personal visions, we sealed the deal in the tradition of the *Code of the West*—with a firm handshake. Color us both delighted!

Finding the Last Dollar

Before we left the guest ranch, I introduced the family to Duane. They unanimously and enthusiastically supported our new partnership and our quest to find the ranch of my extended dream.

We returned to California while Duane set out to accomplish his mission of identifying a ranch that fit our vision and budget. Over the next few weeks, Duane and I would stay in close contact by phone.

Duane's initial task was not simple, nor easy. Find the best ranch real estate agent in the area and then visit and evaluate the ranches that met our criteria. Driving up in his weathered pickup, he would meet with numerous agents and convince them he was representing an interested and qualified buyer—a challenging assignment for anyone with even a new, well-appointed pickup.

During our conversations at the guest ranch Duane had casually mentioned that he was occasionally dating a real estate agent in Montrose. I mentally registered a concern. After a few weeks, Duane called to say his agent search was complete and he had identified the best agent to work with for finding a ranch. His voice telegraphed that he was a bit nervous, then he said he hoped I would not object if his recommendation was a woman.

I sensed he would be suggesting his friend in Montrose—a concern. I was wrong. He had in fact settled on a Nancy Bradburn in Ridgway. He made a great choice. We would eventually buy Last Dollar, Centennial and another open land parcel with Nancy.

After an extended conversation, I agreed to work with his recommendation. Duane and Nancy began to visit all the ranches in the proximity that met our expectations—eliminating some and putting others on a short list for Joan and me to visit as soon as my crammed schedule allowed.

Finally, in late September, I answered a call at the office from Nancy. My first. This was on a Wednesday. She was very direct with only the briefest exchange of pleasantries. She said I was to come out on Friday to see five ranches. I was somewhat aghast—here I was, a senior executive in a global corporation with a demanding and tight personal schedule, I said "I can't make it on such short notice."

She immediately replied, "I thought you wanted to buy a ranch."

Joan and I arrived Friday evening and checked into a delightful bed-and-breakfast inn in Ouray. At the appointed early hour on Saturday, Duane and Nancy pulled up in a clean suburban driven by her husband, Dan, who obviously had been briefed on his limited role as chauffeur.

The first three ranches we looked at were nice, but not what we were looking for. I was getting concerned. The fourth ranch was at the top of Dallas Divide, some eight miles west of Ridgway at an elevation of over 9,000 feet. On our way up we passed the magnificent Double RL Ranch belonging to Ralph and Ricky Lauren. This ranch of some 16,000 acres is adjacent to the highway and extends to the south all the way to the massive Sneffles Range. It was, and is, the most beautiful ranch in the Untied States, in my opinion.

After several miles driving alongside the RRL's famous post-and-pole boundary fence, we came to Last Dollar Road. Turning south on this gravel county road, the adjacent fence marked the western boundary of Ralph's ranch. Just a mile or so down the road alongside a small creek and a continuous collection of beaver ponds, we rose to the top of Hastings Mesa with its open meadows lined with aspen and scrub oak. From there we entered a dirt track that was to take us to the historic homestead.

It was a gorgeous day with clear blue skies and a few puffy white clouds above the high rock peaks at the western end of the Sneffles Range. A gentle breeze created a flutter in the Aspen leaves, which were displaying all their seasonal finery in magnificent yellows with some red shades interspersed. Looking south, the green, open meadows surrendered to lush aspen groves then eventually gave way to the "black timber" (pine and spruce) on the steep slopes of the range. Finally, at timberline, the rock summits of the peaks soared high towards the clouds. It was, indeed, one of the prettiest places God ever made. Joan and I were in awe.

Chapter 3: Finding the Last Dollar

> I was as excited as I have ever been. The possibilities were endless, and just driving up the track to the homestead, my lifelong dream of a ranch with contented cattle grazing in the meadows, a log-and-stone barn for the horses in the shadow of towering rugged mountains with timber-covered slopes— seemingly close enough to touch—was visualized.

After what seemed an eternity, we reached the rather large homestead. The ranch, without improvements, had been purchased in 1901, and construction of the house and log outbuildings continued for the next two-and-a-half decades. However, by 1989, it had essentially been abandoned for more than 40 years. Life on a ranch at that elevation with 12+ feet of snowfall during the winter proved too much of a trial for the second generation of pioneers. They left it and moved to less harsh climes nearby.

The most prominent structure in the homestead was a Country Victorian two-story house constructed using timber from the ranch and guided by drawings purchased from a Sears Roebuck catalog.

There were 10 log outbuildings of various sizes and shapes serving different ranch needs. Of these, nine were still standing, some precariously, while the horse-and-mule barn had simply given up the fight. After a heavy snow, it had collapsed into a jumbled pile of logs. All the buildings, including the house, were built on dry stacked rocks which were losing the battle to keep the buildings from entering mother earth.

Perhaps most people observing this aging settlement would say it was the ugliest mess they had ever witnessed. To me, however, it was a thing of rare beauty. The hardworking, skilled hands that had created this homestead in this beautiful setting should have their work live to see another century, and be recognized for what it truly was.

I was as excited as I have ever been. The possibilities were endless, and just driving up the track to the homestead, my lifelong dream of a ranch with contented cattle grazing in the meadows, a log-and-stone barn for the horses in the shadow of towering, rugged mountains with timber-covered slopes—seemingly close enough to touch—was visualized. There wasn't a stream off to the left, but this ranch was very close to my vision. No doubt, this was the place!

Within a few minutes of our arrival at the homestead, Dan was unpacking a picnic lunch from the suburban and spreading the blankets on dead grass near the house porch with a view to the mountains. In the meantime the rest of us were inspecting each building. A few minutes later we were enjoying the full menu of skillet-fried chicken (prepared earlier that morning), potato salad, baked beans and homemade bread with iced tea. For dessert, we had an apple pie (baked the day before). Nancy knew how to host a country picnic. Life couldn't get much better!

Conversation was loud and animated, but I detected a hesitant enthusiasm from Nancy. When pressed, she informed us she had the listing on this ranch (no problem!). Then she let us know she was negotiating with a serious buyer—a lawyer from Phoenix (a problem). Okay. I thought, so we have only one buyer to beat. Doable!!

Earlier that morning, during the breakfast portion of our bed-and-breakfast accommodation, I had attempted to outline my negotiating strategy to Joan. When we would look at a property, I suggested Joan politely point out aspects that gave her concern, but she should refrain from showing enthusiasm if or when she thought a property would be suitable for us—this, of course, to assure a stronger negotiating posture.

She asked, "What if I see the ideal ranch, how do I communicate that to you?" I simply said we would need a password. Joan suggested "beaver" to let me know this was the place. Good plan.

During our picnic, Joan asked Nancy, "Are there any beavers here?" A somewhat perplexed Nancy said that there were beavers in the creek nearby, but none close to the homestead. To which Joan replied, "I love beavers—can we see any beavers?" We all agreed we would make a special effort on our way out to spot some beavers along the country road. Joan gave me a concerned look to see if I had picked up on her subtle signal.

On Sunday morning after mass, we again joined Nancy and Duane to look at the last ranch near Telluride that comprised Nancy's short list. Joan, Duane and I were pre-occupied, so we cut the tour short and went to Nancy's office in Ridgway to prepare a serious offer. The rest is history. My dream was going to become a reality—as were Joan's and Duane's.

A Brief History of Last Dollar Ranch

Author's Note:

When we acquired the Last Dollar Ranch, one of our early objectives was to document its rich history and the accomplishments of the hard-working, dedicated people who created it. For that task, we turned to Dona Freeman, historian and genealogist, who for the previous eight years had been employed at the Montrose Daily Press *as history editor. There she enjoyed a large and appreciative following for her weekly columns on local history.*

Dona readily accepted our commission and, with considerable skill and enthusiasm, set about collecting pictures and documents from the elderly, early ranch pioneers. These she augmented with detailed interviews.

In 1993, we self-published (through our Double Shoe Publishing Company) her book Last Dollar Ranch. *It was hugely popular with the families featured and with the local population. Copies of the first edition were eventually depleted, so in 2005 we printed an expanded second edition, which likewise has all been distributed. Much of the content of this chapter has been extracted from those books.*

After we purchased the Centennial Ranch from the Smith brothers, Dona collected a trove of items from the extended Smith families, and in 1992, we published Dona's book, Smith Ranch – Colona, Colorado 1879-1992. *I draw from this book much of the material for Chapter Nine: A Brief History of Centennial.*

I am extremely grateful to Dona for her great work in preserving the story of these historic ranches.

T he earliest white men to set foot in the high valley we now call Last Dollar Ranch were the mountain men, the likes of Jim Bridger, in search of beaver pelts to satisfy demand from the East and England for quality top hats. They set their winter trap lines in this area from about 1810 to 1850. A considerable number of beaver still call the adjacent Leopard Creek home.

The first written ownership of the valley was Sam Nesbitt, who paid 1888 taxes of $9.31 and in 1889, paid delinquent taxes of $25.13. His sole interest in the land was to harvest timber and supply cross ties for the construction, in 1890-1893, of the 3'6' narrow-gauge railroad between Ridgway and Telluride.

Oil painting on the Last Dollar ranch by Ted Moews

In 1901, two brothers scraped together a down payment and purchased the property from Nesbitt. Andrew Boyd (Boyd) and Johnson Ezekiel (Johns) Collins borrowed $1,000 from their parents, Hasten and Martha Collins. Boyd and Johns used the borrowed money for a down payment on the agreed $3,300 purchase price of the Nesbitt place, which included all the implements and tools.

Boyd assumed the title and Johns homesteaded a 160-acre adjacent parcel to the south. They further expanded with a 160-acre homestead. In 1910, they bought another 160 acres a mile to the west.

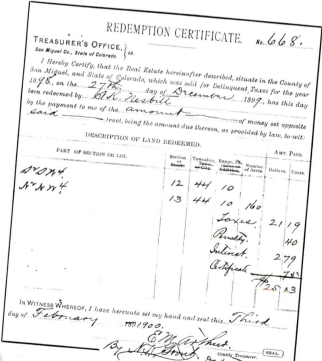

THE COLLINS BROTHERS

ANDREW BOYD COLLINS

JOHNSON EZEKIEL COLLINS

> It was a hard life starting a ranch and dairy at this altitude, but remarkably, they persevered.

Their first building project in 1901 was a log house. The picture below was taken in 1906 of the house with Martha Collins (the cook), the brothers, Will Watts (the hired man), dogs and the anti-social hired man sitting behind the stump.

It was a hard life starting a ranch and dairy at this altitude, but remarkably, they persevered.

Long summer days were spent digging ditches and irrigating their grain and hay fields, putting up hay for winter feed and constructing log outbuildings for horses, mules, milk cows, calves, pigs and chickens. All field work was performed with draft horses.

Breaking ground for a grain field was with a team and all transportation was accomplished with saddle horses. Water came from hand-dug wells about three feet in diameter. Cutting and splitting aspen logs for fuel was a long fall chore to provide household heat during the brutal winter months.

The image to the right illustrates how hardy these people were. Will was the hired hand who met Edith when she helped cook at the ranch for the summer crew. Readers are reminded that the buggy trip, one way, from the ranch to Montrose was some 35 miles.

HIRED MAN TAKES A DAY OFF to go get married on June 24, 1908. Will Watts was united in marriage to Edith Caddy on this day. On their wedding day they rode horseback to Noel, where they borrowed a horse and buggy from a loving old couple, the Gallaghers, and drove to Montrose to be married by Judge Haney. They had their picture taken in their rumpled wedding finery before returning to Hastings Mesa that same day. Friends predicted that 20 year old Will and 18 year old Edith would not stay married. (Seventy-seven years later the devoted couple died within 15 days of each other.)

Chapter 4: A Brief History of Last Dollar Ranch

During those early decades at the ranch, they would occasionally play as hard as they worked.

One common complaint of the women attending these dances was that many of the men would get falling-down drunk with just enough time and energy to do the milking the next morning after a long ride in the back of the buggy going home.

Two early, significant events occurred in close proximity to one another. Johns died of a brain tumor in 1911, just a few months after Boyd married Gertrude "Gertie" Sanders.

THE MARRIAGE IS FORTHCOMING of these two Western Colorado residents. Gertrude Eugenia Saunders, the daughter of Charles O'Bannon and Elizabeth Marie "Sadie" (Biebush) Saunders, and Andrew Boyd Collins, the son of Martha Jane (Moore) Collins and Hasten Collins, son of Elijah and Margy Collins, were married on August 22, 1911, and made their home on the Collins Brothers ranch on Hastings Mesa in San Miguel County, Colorado.

The receipt dated 2 April 1912 from the Placerville Store gives the reader some idea of what groceries were needed to augment the beef, pork, chicken, eggs, milk and potatoes that were produced on the ranch. These provisions were paid for with money from cream sales—the primary cash crop.

Getting the stacking done on the Collins' Ranch are Jessie Taylor leading the stacker horse, George Taylor stacking and Boyd Collins on the Go Devil.

The ranch slowly became more established and modernized.

In 1915, they decided to build a proper house with timber from the ranch. Drawings for a Country Victorian were ordered from a Sears Roebuck catalog.

Logs from the ranch going to a nearby sawmill to be cut into lumber for the new house.

On the porch of the new house.

A wood shed adjacent to the house, was constructed in 1923 for the sole purpose of keeping wood dry and handy for winter cooking and heating. This was the last of 10 log outbuildings built at the homestead.

Left, the wood shed

Below left, cutting aspen logs to be split and stored in the wood shed.

Below, a bridal shower at the ranch in 1936.

People in the west have long recorded events by carving in the soft bark of aspen trees, which then become preserved for the life of the tree. The hard-working men and women who carved the Last Dollar Ranch out of the wilderness left today's generation with interesting tidbits about their daily lives.

At the upper end of the meadow just south of the homestead is a large grove of aspen. Many of the trees were well over 50 years old with a diameter of at least 12 inches when the Collins brothers first arrived in 1901.

The workers at Last Dollar took this tree-carving practice to new heights, as there are more than a hundred trees on the ranch recording various events. Many of the carvings have been recorded and photographed as they remain legible until the tree dies—some up to an age of 200 years.

Normally the bark artist would carve his initials (ABC for Boyd and JEC for Johns) at the top and the date next. During the early years, this was all that was recorded, but later a variety of events were added. These would include such activities shown here as they were carved:

- ERIGATING WHEAT
- CUTING HAY
- TURNED WATER IN DITCH!
- WORK ON DITCH - TICKLED TO DEATH
- CUTTING BARLEY - FINE BARLEY
- LOOKS RAINY AS HELL
- GETTING SNOW TO MAKE ICE CREAM
- PUTTING IN HEADGATE
- REBUILDING FENCE - GETTING POSTS
- HUNTING HORSES
- TURNED ALL WATER ON. DRY AND HOT. NO RAIN TO DO ANY GOOD
- FINISHED DRILLING THIS PATCH IN TIMOTHY
- THE LORD IS MY SHEPARD
- RAIN, RAIN, DAM YOU RAIN

- HERDING SHEEP
- EVERETT COLLINS & STELLA DUNCAN WERE MARRIED 1936
- PULLED MARTIN TRAPS
- FIRST HORSE FLY
- JUST RIDING AROUND, ABOUT READY TO STORM
- TWO BIG BEAR PASSED JUST NOW
- ROLLING WIRE FOR DITCH FENCE ON GRAIN HILL
- PULLING STUMPS
- DEER HUNTING - NO LUCK
- HUNTING CATTLE - ONE GONE YET
- TAKING A VIEW OF THE MOST BEAUTIFUL RANCH IN THE WORLD
- BEAR
- CHASING LLOYD'S HORSES

Chapter 4: A Brief History of Last Dollar Ranch

Here are pictures of a few of the carvings.

JEC
Oct 27
1901

JEC
June 27
1904

ABC
MAY 27, 1918
BOUGHT A DODGE
TRUCK TODAY
BY GOD

As of this writing, this 1917 Dodge truck sits in Boyd's granddaughter's Montrose garage and is still in running condition.

Volume 4: The Golden Years

ABC
V. CAIN
JULY 20,
1933
SET BEAR
TRAP

COT
NOTHING
(Was probably added later by someone else.)

Bear claw marks are on the side of the tree.

(Southeast of house)

ABC
OUR FATHER
DIED APRIL 2,
1947

When we purchased the ranch in 1989, our family continued the tradition of carving on the aspen trees. Our son-in-law, Jan Gundersen, proposed to our daughter, Natascha, by carving the proposal on a tree then inviting her for a walk on snowshoes to the tree.

The fresh carving reads, "NMK - Will you marry me? JSG" They were married on the ranch 5 July 2003.

Chapter 4: A Brief History of Last Dollar Ranch

> Once the homestead and surrounding acreage lost its full-time residents in 1947, it started its inevitable decline. The land was leased on single-year terms for sheep and cattle grazing. But, because of the short lease periods, the renters had little incentive to irrigate or maintain the fences, hence it was overgrazed and fell into continuing disrepair.

The hard, but satisfying life continued on the ranch through the Great Depression and World War II. The cash crop was cream, delivered by wagon to the railroad siding at Noel, some two miles away, and then by train to Ridgway or Telluride. About 45 cows were milked by hand twice a day in the large cow barn, which lacked heat and lighting. The milk and cream were then separated using a hand-cranked separator. Beef, pork and eggs were also sold to help the ranch prosper, but it was indeed a tough life.

Boyd died April 2, 1947. Not long after he passed, his heirs declared they were tired of the demanding work and trying winters. The land was divided and deeded to Boyd's children. Eventually the homestead portion was passed on to Boyd's son, Dee, who in time gave equal portions to his two sons and daughter, LaVelle Collins Corey. The boys quickly sold their land, but LaVelle retained her portion, and bought out some of her brothers' holdings.

Once the homestead and surrounding acreage lost its full-time residents in 1947, it started its inevitable decline. The land was leased on single-year terms for sheep and cattle grazing. But, because of the short lease periods, the renters had little incentive to irrigate or maintain the fences, hence it was overgrazed and fell into continuing disrepair.

In September 1989, Joan and I shared our exquisite picnic on the ranch and silently declared we must purchase the ranch, renovate the physical facilities and preserve it for future generations. It was a mission we accepted—the place deserved no less.

Cream Separator

Volume 4: The Golden Years

Saving the Last Dollar

This painting, a gift from Nancy Bradburn (our real estate agent), shows the homestead entrance when we discovered it.

The task of cleaning up the ranch and restoring the buildings was formidable—almost incomprehensible. As the old saying goes, "How do you eat an elephant?" The answer is, "One bite at a time."

The entire ranch had suffered more than 40 years of near abandonment with no one resident to continue the needed constant maintenance in such a harsh environment. However, I could clearly visualize the final product of the restoration effort, so when the snow cleared in the spring of 1990, we took our first bite of the elephant.

> I could clearly visualize the final product of the restoration effort, so when the snow cleared in the spring of 1990, we took our first bite of the elephant.

Three people deserve the lion's share of credit for this restoration:

- **Duane Beamer** (book dedication) who was there every day, all day, to supervise all the jobs, manage getting the material and extra help needed, all the while wearing his tool belt.

- **Ted Moews** (book dedication) was the thinker, bringing years of accumulated talent and experience to bear on how to salvage the log outbuildings and prepare them for another century of survival.

- **Howard McCall** (recipient of the dedication of our earlier book, ***A Heritage in Iron***) worked from rough sketches by Duane and Ted to create detailed ironwork drawings. Then, he'd either forge the array of hinges, latches, hooks, sconces, etc., himself or farm the blacksmithing out to his highly skilled artisan friends.

It worked. By summer 1990 the transformation was well underway.

Ranchland

To restore production in the hay meadows, repairing the irrigation system was essential. This might sound simple, but that system consists of the head gate, flumes and a two-mile-long dedicated ditch that delivers the precious water to the fields.

Rusty barbed-wire perimeter fences as well as the interior cross-fences were not only unsalvageable, but a hazard to wildlife and future livestock. Some of the wire was completely buried and had to be pulled out of the ground with a tractor or winch, then disposed of.

Many large aspen trees on the southern boundary had fallen and needed to be cleared before fences could be replaced with "zig-zag" or "worm" fences made from lodge poles with vertical aspen stays. These fences, although labor intensive to build, were placed on the surface of the ground without any requirement to dig postholes. They not only could be constructed entirely with local materials, but also best survived the heavy snow loads where in the winter one might walk over the fence wearing snowshoes.

Then there was the sizable task of clearing dead trees and a sea of fallen branches from what would become the 30-acre "night pasture" for our horses next to the envisioned log and stone barn.

For that assignment, Duane hired a recent local high school graduate, a true patriot with a remarkable work ethic. His name was Scott Fox and his ambition was to become a Navy Seal. After a year working for Duane, he indeed did become a highly decorated Seal, a position in which he served honorably for the next 20 years.

We re-seeded the hay meadows that once again became highly productive.

> We now were smarter, and with one significant procedure modification, we were able to tackle the restoration of the other eight log outbuildings.

Outbuildings

When we commenced our restoration efforts at Last Dollar, there were nine log outbuildings still standing against the wind and heavy snow in various stages of deterioration and near collapse. One, the original horse-and-mule barn, had given up the struggle and was nothing but a large pile of weathered logs.

What to do? We devised a plan, starting with the smallest building, a tool shed, to jack the intact building off its sinking, dry-stacked rock foundation high enough to form and place sound concrete foundations. This was awkward and could be hazardous, but with such a small structure, we persevered.

Once the foundation was complete we lowered the building onto its invisible foundation. Next, we removed any rotten logs, replacing them with sound logs salvaged from the barn pile. With the walls structurally strong, we then removed the roof exposing the rafters, making repairs as needed. A 3/4" plywood roof was then secured onto the rafters. Finally, cedar shake shingles were carefully nailed in place. The result: A strong, functional structure that, with minimal maintenance, could resist the harsh environment for at least another century.

We now were smarter, and with one significant procedure modification, we were able to tackle the restoration of the other eight log outbuildings. The change was to borrow jacks, large steel beams and heavy-duty skates from a local house mover. The new plan was to jack the building up several feet, install the long steel beams under the structure, then lower the building onto the skates to move it clear of its old site. We could then place the concrete foundation, slide the building back over it, lower the building back onto the foundation and proceed with all the subsequent operations we had perfected on the small tool shed.

They say a picture is worth a thousand words, so in the next few pages, I will simply illustrate this work on several buildings with a "then and now" title indicating the original and current uses.

THEN and NOW

Tool Shed (1903) - Tool Shed (present)

THEN and NOW

Garage Shop (1921) - Carpenter Shop (present)

THEN and NOW

Hog Barn (1906) - Equipment Barn (present)

Chapter 5: Saving the Last Dollar

THEN and NOW

Chicken House (1903) - Bunk House (present)

35

THEN and NOW

Calf Barn (1904) - Equipment Shed (present)

Chapter 5: Saving the Last Dollar

THEN and NOW

Cow Barn (1903) - Cow Barn (present)

Volume 4: The Golden Years

Wood Shed (1923) - Guest House (present)

Chapter 5: Saving the Last Dollar

So! You now get the picture of the log outbuilding restoration.

The House

In the tradition of the Old West, a pioneer rancher should keep his development priorities right. First, he should build shelter and fences to protect his livestock. Secondly, he should provide adequate facilities for his hired help. Then, and only then, should he focus on more comfortable quarters for himself and his family.

By 1915, Boyd Collins decided that with the last few good years of cream and beef sales, it was indeed time to address building a comfortable house. Mind you, without electricity or running water, the modern version of "comfortable" may not fully apply here.

The first task was to secure the lumber. On the rising slopes within a mile of the homestead were stately, sound spruce trees. The first chore, reserved for the relatively quiet days of winter, was to fell those trees and haul them by horse-drawn sleds to a primitive, but adequate sawmill a couple miles away.

Once cut into sized pieces, the lumber was "stacked and stickered" then left to dry naturally for two years.

The next step was to select the type and size of house to be constructed. Popular at the time were "Country Victorian" Houses with an adequate selection of plans available from the Sears Roebuck catalog—always present in western country households (with the added benefit of being transferred to the outhouse with the arrival of a new edition).

Chapter 5: Saving the Last Dollar

Boyd and Gertie made their selection and ordered the construction drawings from the catalog. In the fall of 1916, with hay for winter feed cut and stacked, the house project commenced.

Mind you, when completed, it looked grand with its two stories and a wrap-around porch, but budget constraints necessitated a few comfort cuts. Perhaps the most significant was to eliminate the insulation in the floors, walls and ceilings. That was unfortunate, for during the high-country winters, you really need to keep the cold outside. With only split aspen blocks for fuel in the oven and heating stove, it was virtually impossible to retain heat in the north portion of the house. So, in winter months only about two-thirds of the house was habitable.

Charles Dee Collins was born on July 14, 1917 at the recently completed home of his parents on Hastings Mesa.

Of course, in their haste to build the house, the foundation drudgery was expedited by using dry-stacked field stones.

The house was completed in 1917, then virtually abandoned some three decades later when Boyd died and his family voted to move to warmer nearby winter climes.

We entered the picture some four decades after the Collins family had abandoned ship. The house was still a beautiful structure, although showing signs of age and abuse from the elements.

Not unlike the log outbuildings, we would restore the house to its original splendor, while also adding the creature comforts of a solid foundation, a crawl space, running water, electricity, and thick insulation as well as in-floor heating. The objective was to create a modern, comfortable home while retaining the identical exterior appearance of the house as originally constructed. This we accomplished—the only visible modern convenience being a pizza-sized satellite dish on the roof.

Our restoration procedure had been perfected on the outbuildings: jack it up, move it away to enable us to complete the foundations and buried utilities, then set it down on the new foundation so we could work on the structure above.

Chapter 5: Saving the Last Dollar

Today, this beautiful century-old Country Victorian house stands as a testament to what can be achieved to preserve our great, but fading, Western Heritage.

New Barn

Having restored the log outbuildings and the house, our next major project was to construct a horse barn to provide shelter and hay storage for our equine friends that would compliment the other structures of the homestead.

For the initial task of design, we naturally turned to our good and talented friend who had designed and built several barns, Ted Moews, and by this time had made a very significant investment of time and effort in saving the Last Dollar.

In keeping with its surroundings, I favored the construction of a functional log and stone barn. It would be a formidable task, but one worth the time and effort. In pencil sketches, Ted created several options. The one elected is illustrated here.

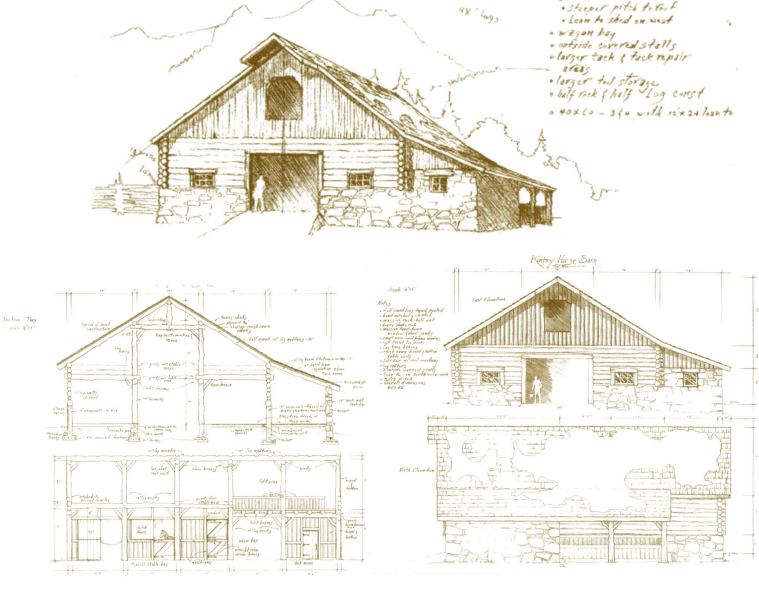

Work began immediately for a solid concrete foundation.

Chapter 5: Saving the Last Dollar

The completed barn soon became home to our handsome team of Belgian draft horses and our saddle horses, as well as a tack room, leather shop and feed room.

Chapter 5: Saving the Last Dollar

49

Volume 4: The Golden Years

Chapter 5: Saving the Last Dollar

The completed barn not only served the needs of our men and horses, but also has been featured in national magazines and has proven to be a magnet for commercial photo shoots including ads for Marlboro, Budweiser's Clydesdales along with fashion and automotive ads.

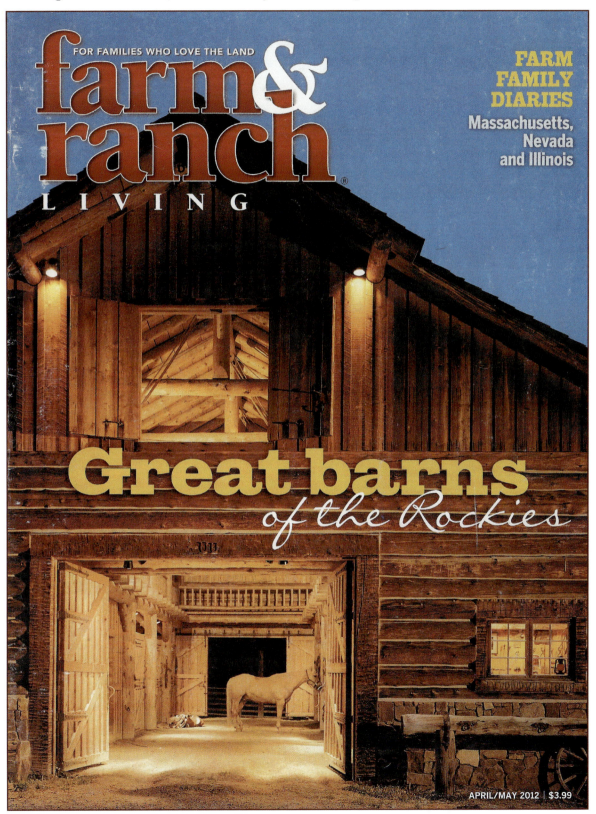

Ironwork

The following text and images are from our book, A Ranching Legacy, by Rafael Routson.

"Heavy, functioning ironwork accents the log-and-stone barn and restored log buildings on Last Dollar Ranch. Strap hinges, tapered and twisted lever latches, and cane bolts allow the plank doors to swing easily and fasten open or closed. Hand-forged arrowhead hangers allow the back doors to slide open, even when snow drifts press against the doors. In the barn, detailed latches close the Dutch stall doors. Ted Moews drew multiple designs for artistic, functional iron hardware. Vince and Ted selected an arrowhead motif and incorporated the design into the hinges, hangers, lever latches, and tie rings of the Last Dollar buildings. Glenn Gilmore, of Gilmore Metalsmithing in Hamilton, Montana, and Howard McCall, Stoneywall Forge in Greenville, South Carolina, collaborated on the forge work. They hand-forged each piece, combining detailed designing and drafting with skilled forge work to produce the iron hardware.

Howard McCall

Glen Gilmore

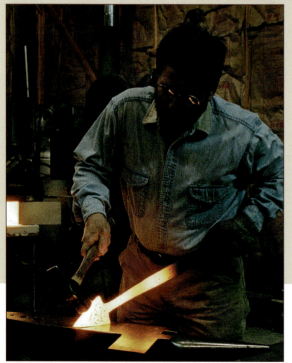

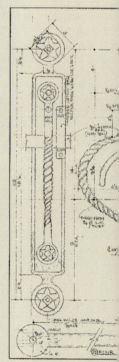

Howard McCall designed and forged the lever latches, cane bolts, numerous hooks and eyes, and cross-tie rings. Glenn forged the arrowhead hinges, hangers, hooks, window hinges and keepers, and the latches for the stall doors. All ironwork embodies the exceptional artistic eyes, craftsmanship, and individuality of the designer and blacksmiths."

The art and skill of blacksmithing emerged six thousand years ago, and functioned as an essential part of cultural development in all parts of the world. Blacksmithing evolved differently in various locations, though the basic techniques and methods of ironworking were principally the same. Blacksmiths on several continents developed techniques for working the hot iron, and they contributed to a collective body of knowledge that was passed down through generations.

Chapter 5: Saving the Last Dollar

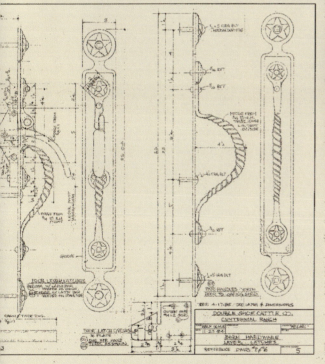

Blacksmiths played an integral part in the exploration and settling of early America; they made and repaired wagons, carpentry tools, mining and logging tools, household necessities, and farming equipment. The larger towns and port cities had specialized smiths to forge parts for ships and railroads. Each farm and ranch had a forge of some kind, and many early ranchers and pioneers had a fundamental understanding of metal work.

Volume 4: The Golden Years

Chapter 5: Saving the Last Dollar

The Gates, Corrals and Pole Fences
Finally, our last construction effort was to contract with a colorful, hard-working fence builder named Chuck Cordova, who, with his extended-family crew, would build the pole fences and corrals necessary to hold and work our cattle. He would also construct the entrance gate to our homestead.

We needed a gate at the entrance of the ranch from the county road. My criteria for the gate to Ted for the design was: "Because it would frame the massive mountains just beyond the homestead, a wimpy gate simply would not be appropriate."

I have always been sensitive to the Texas putdown of boasting individuals as, "All hat and no cattle." Here in the mountains we say, "The smaller the ranch, the bigger the gate." Last Dollar was admittedly a small spread, therefore, we needed a massive gate. Ted didn't disappoint.

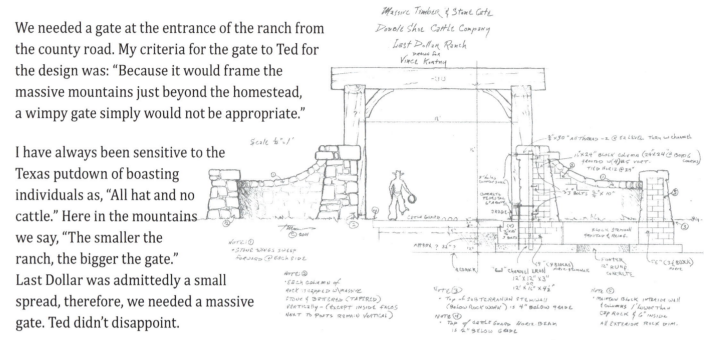

The Pond

Once the restoration of the land and existing buildings was complete, and the new barn loft was stacked with hay for the horses, we turned our attention to building a stock pond to capture the spring runoff. It would add to the esthetics of the ranch, provide water for our livestock and hopefully provide year-round habitat for mountain trout. It did, magnificently, all those things.

As usual, our first move was to reach out to Ted Moews for guidance and inspiration. He sat down a few hundred yards from the homestead with a clear view of the buildings, the meadows, the timbered slopes beyond, and finally, the rocky peaks rising majestically to the clouds. He sat there, with his pencil and pad, studying the low ground contours, and slowly created the outline of a pond of some three acres as it would be if it was entirely God-made.

Arms of the pond would extend into the natural drainage ditches, a small island with willow-covered shores and spruce trees in the middle would be created on the south side of the pond close to the homestead. The retaining dirt dam would be low, with irregular gentle slopes covered with native alpine grass. An outlet pipe was buried in the event the pond ever needed to be drained, or to provide an ample emergency water supply in the event of a fire. In time, no visitor would ever guess it was a man-made pond.

A deep and wide trench was cut in the bottom of the pond to provide a safe haven for trout during the winter with the excavated material used to slightly elevate an all-weather access road from the county road to the homestead.

Volume 4: The Golden Years

"Located near the jagged peaks of the Sneffels Range, Last Dollar Ranch is a 392-acre spread that borders a 13,000-acre property owned by clothing magnate Ralph Lauren. Last Dollar Ranch has fields of wildflowers, irrigated meadows and groves of aspen where deer, elk, bear and other wildlife live. There is also a three-acre trout pond. During the last 20 years, the ranch has been used as a location for national advertising campaigns for Anheuser-Busch, Coors and Marlboro. –**Forbes Magazine, 10/12/2001**

The Completion Celebration

Once all the work described in this chapter was complete, it was time to celebrate the accomplishment.

We would hold an old-fashioned, outdoor barbecue at the ranch. Everyone who had worked on the ranch, be they laborers on the fence crew, carpenters, truck drivers, blacksmiths, et. al., were invited to come and to bring their families to show them what had been accomplished and their specific role in the effort. Friends and neighbors also came at our invitation, illustrated by Ted Moews.

To show our appreciation to everyone who has helped with the restoration of our beautiful ranch and to celebrate July 4th together with our friends and neighbors, you and your family are invited to an old-fashioned barbecue at the Last Dollar Ranch.

Date: July 4, 1991

Time: Between 2 and 6 p.m.

We're hoping you'll be able to join us.

Duane Beamer
Joan and Vince Kontny

Thanks to the skill, creativity and hard work of so many great people, collectively, we did save Last Dollar.

Volume 4: The Golden Years

Protection in Perpetuity
"As Long as the Grass Grows and the Rivers Flow"

You may not be familiar with the quote in this chapter title, so let me take an uneducated and poorly researched shot at an explanation as it applies to Last Dollar Ranch.

Some individual with unverified credentials states the language was first used in a peace treaty promised to the Cherokee nation by the state of Georgia in 1820 to end violence regarding land occupied by the tribe. Of course, history will record that the treaty, despite the language, didn't last all that long.

The government tried again when one faction of the Cherokee leadership signed a treaty selling their Cherokee land to Georgia and agreed to move west by 1838. Supposedly, the Cherokee council unanimously rejected the treaty, but the senate in Washington ratified it.

This, of course, led to the infamous "Trail of Tears" as some 18,000 Cherokees were displaced and moved to the "Indian Territory" further west; perhaps with the same promise for occupying their new home. Still other scholars of Indian history say the words were also used in treaties with plains Indians later in the century.

Whatever, I like the phrase because it represents in easy-to-understand words what the white man of that day, and today, simply call "in perpetuity"—"unlimited time, eternity." So how does this relate to Last Dollar Ranch?

As I have repeatedly stated, the high mountain valley of Last Dollar Ranch is one of the prettiest places God ever made. Joan and I were in total agreement that it should be protected for all future generations from any development, hopefully to avoid the alarming breakup of local historic ranches for development and recreation by the wealthy few.

Conservation Easement

Shortly after acquiring Last Dollar and while the renovations were still in progress, I began a search for applicable means of legal protection. To my delight, such a program was in existence; although few in the legal field were even aware of it. My early inquiries to Colorado lawyers resulted in only one in more than 20 being familiar with the term "conservation easement," let alone how to implement one. Eventually, I located the help I needed to proceed.

So what is a conservation easement? It is a power invested in a qualified land conservation organization (land trust) for a specified land area to achieve a stated conservation purpose. It is an interest in real property with an agreement between the land owner and the land trust to achieve certain conservation objectives. The agreement is recorded in land records and its restrictions "run with the land"—i.e. in perpetuity, or as otherwise understood, "as long as the grass grows and the rivers flow."

With a knowledgeable and experienced lawyer in Denver, we selected American Farmland Trust, Inc., a District of Columbia nonprofit corporation, as the land trust to whom we would donate our easement. They were one of the largest and most professional such organizations in the United States at the time. Their specialty was protecting farmland threatened by urban expansion, but they felt comfortable working to protect a western ranch.

The Devil is in the Details

The lawyer guided us on whatever was required before we could obtain a conservation easement. We needed a detailed and accurate legal description of Last Dollar Ranch, including any easements for access or irrigation ditches. This necessitated a survey to identify boundaries and any easements to create a final plat.

Once completed, we then had to search the land title history, not only to confirm the surface rights, but the sub-surface mineral rights as well. In our case, this was a problem. When Boyd Collins divided the ranch and gifted it to his heirs, and they subsequently to their heirs, the mineral rights somehow dropped through the cracks and remained with the early heirs.

We, therefore, had to identify mineral rights, which were not included in our purchase, track down the owners of those rights and then purchase such rights. The likelihood of any subsurface mineral deposits existing at the ranch were slim to none, but the legal owners of the rights wanted to squeeze every last dollar out of their historic holdings, so purchase negotiations were difficult and protracted, but eventually successful.

The next hurdle was to complete a detailed "baseline inventory and description" by a qualified biologist. This study necessitated the identification of the geographical setting and the description of all "conservation values" such as:

- soil
- vegetation
- wildlife
- agriculture
- cultural
- scenic

Chapter 6: Protection in Perpetuity

Once that work was completed, we required an appraisal by a qualified real estate appraiser with experience working on ranch land conservation easements.

The purpose of the appraisal was to quantify the value of the property "before conveyance of the easement" and "after conveyance of the easement." The difference between the two being the "market value of the conservation easement." In 1994, when we donated the conservation easement for Last Dollar Ranch to the American Farmland Trust, the only financial benefit to us, the donor, was a tax deduction in the amount of the market value, the same deduction any taxpayer was entitled to by donating funds to a qualified 501(c)3 organization, such as a church or school, as a charitable gift.

Finally, American Farmland Trust required a substantial cash donation to cover the cost of monitoring the easement in the future.

Once we had jumped through all the hoops, the Deed of Conservation Easement was granted on 4 November 1994.

63

> It is extremely satisfying to know, with certainty,
> that for future generations decades from now,
> the Last Dollar Ranch will be much the same as
> it exists today.

In the decades since our donation, Colorado has passed legislation with far more extensive tax benefits—and even the ability to sell those benefits to third parties, all in an attempt to make it more financially attractive for landowners to protect open land from development.

In the documents, we had identified an agricultural building envelope containing the homestead and a separate residential building envelope in the event we, or a future owner, would want to build a house.

The Deed of Conservation Easement describes:

What one can do:

- Fences may be repaired and replaced
- New buildings and other structures and improvements to be used for agricultural purposes may be built within the agricultural building envelope
- Two new single-family residential dwellings may be built within the residential building envelopes
- Conduct all farming operations in accordance with the conservation plan
- Retain and reserve the use of water rights

What one cannot do:

- Divide or subdivide the property
- Harvest timber except for firewood and domestic uses
- Mine or extract soil, sand, gravel, rock, oil, natural gas, fuel or any other mineral substance
- Pave with concrete, asphalt or any other paving material
- Dump or accumulate any kind of trash or refuse
- Construct any golf courses, airstrips or helicopter pads
- Fail to provide proper upkeep and maintenance

The entire process and subsequent documentation of the conservation easement satisfied the objectives Joan and I had established initially. Those objectives were simply to provide in perpetuity:

- Open space
- Wildlife habitat
- Agriculture production

It is extremely satisfying to know, with certainty, that for future generations decades from now, the Last Dollar Ranch will be much the same as it exists today.

A Day in the Life of the Last Dollar Ranch—Circa 1935

Introduction

As I write this, and as most read this, we are surrounded by the comforts and conveniences of life in the 21st century. Most people today, in all likelihood, have little if any idea just how hard the early pioneers in the Colorado mountains worked to make a life for themselves and their families.

The 1930s were tough times in rural America with the country racked by the devastating Great Depression, and the Great Plains trying to survive a serious drought. On the plains, huge dust storms were the unintended consequence of tilling the rich prairie soil and thus breaking up the buffalo grass that for eons had held the soil and its intermittent moisture in place.

Life on what was then known simply as "the Collins Place" was better than that of their agricultural counterparts in the flat plains to the east—better because in a period with no 7-Elevens or Wal-Marts, these people made do with what they could produce, create or fix. They were so very self-reliant. However, few people worked harder than these God-fearing, Bible-reading, patriotic souls. Life was not easy.

In an effort to provide the reader a little exposure to these people and their struggle to survive and prosper, I enlisted the help of:

- Duane Beamer, who lived on the ranch for 25 years after we acquired it; and

- Ted Moews, who built his log cabin 35 years ago just a mile south of the homestead as the crow flies and lives there to this day.

I sat down with Duane and Ted one afternoon and we sketched out what would have been a day's activity in the winter and again in the summer during the mid-1930s. Apologies are extended in advance for any inaccuracies that may exist from my lack of research in this narrative.

Winter

When: Wednesday, 6 February 1935

Where: The Collins Place on top of Dallas Divide, elevation 9,300'

The temperature at night would be ±10° Fahrenheit (it was "cold as hell" and no one paid much attention to the thermometer reading). Depending on the sunshine, it could be above freezing during the day.

There would be four to five feet of snow on the ground (average annual snowfall exceeded 12 feet) but it was impossible to measure since a breeze or strong wind was constant, piling the snow in drifts around buildings and blowing off barren ground to settle in the forest of aspen and spruce.

Sunrise was 7:11 a.m. in neighboring Ridgway, sunset at 5:40 p.m. A short day was made even shorter at the Collins Place because of the high ridge to the east and another ridge to the west.

In the country Victorian house were the parents, Boyd and Gertie, and their four children in their late teens and early 20s. The girls, Fern and Grace, shared a bedroom upstairs on the south side. The boys, Dee and Everett, were in the other upstairs bedroom, again on the south side.

Because the house was built in 1917 without any insulation, the two upstairs bedrooms on the north side, as well as the main-floor bedroom below were simply closed the entire winter as they were impossible to heat. It was cold inside, but no pipes would freeze (because there were no pipes).

At 3:45 a.m., Boyd and Gertie would wake, as they did every day throughout the year. Milking would start at 4 a.m., rain or shine, summer or winter. Gertie or Boyd had already been up several times during the night, about every two hours, to add wood on the coals in the kitchen stove as well as in the pot-bellied stove in the dining room. These two stoves were the only sources of heat in the house and they shared a common chimney.

A call would alert the kids who would reluctantly roll out from under their piles of blankets and quickly get dressed. Dee and Everett would pull on heavy, well-darned socks, but no shoes. This was basically a "no shoes" house, in an effort to keep the floors clean. Outside boots were placed on two gunnysacks just inside the kitchen door. If hunger pangs caused one to forget to remove his shoes when he entered the house, he should be prepared to duck the flat side of an iron skillet that would be swung at his head.

Winter outhouse

Chapter 7: A Day in the Life of the Last Dollar Ranch—Circa 1935

Two-seater with the Montgomery Ward catalog

There was a scramble to use the outhouse, a respectable three-holer designed for papa bear, mama bear and baby bear. Inside the outhouse was last year's Montgomery Ward catalog, which served two purposes—one was to provide something to read (during the winter this luxury was seldom used for that purpose).

There was a well-established routine for early morning outhouse etiquette. One would simply lean out the kitchen door and give a loud holler. If it was answered from the direction of the outhouse, you waited, if not, you could proceed. The outhouse was located close to the house, but not too close.

Morning Milking

A hired man would soon appear at the house from the very small bunkhouse just a few yards away. Soon Boyd and one of his sons, this day it was Everett, would emerge from the house to join the hired man. All were similarly dressed with lace-up rubberized boots, either heavy cotton or woolen trousers, a layer of wool underwear and shirts topped off with a weathered, lined denim coat. A worn hat would cover the head, but usually not the ears.

From the small separator room on the porch adjacent to the kitchen door, each would grab a number of milk buckets. Gertie handed Everett a single bucket with warm soapy water and a rag. Each man would light a railroad lantern, then off he went into the darkness for the 40-yard trek to the cow barn.

They walked single file in the same packed snow track they used for every trip to and from the barn—up and over the snowdrifts that covered the ground.

Meantime, Gertie, Fern and Grace had lit more oil lamps in the kitchen and dining room. The lamps could burn either lamp oil or kerosene. Lamp oil burned clean but was relatively expensive. Kerosene smoked a little, but was cheap and readily available. So, what the hell, they only used kerosene.

Dee would stay in the house to replenish the split wood for the kitchen wood stove and the pot-bellied stove. Two stacks of wood in the woodshed were kept separate for their specific purposes (smaller wood for the oven—larger for the living room stove). Once finished with the wood chore, Dee would be given another job in the house—on this day it was to make a good quantity of butter in the large stoneware butter churn. Cream agitation was created with a pole inserted through the lid of the churn and then vigorously plunged up and down until the cream had separated into butter and buttermilk, which was then drained off.

Butter churn

The men reached the cow barn, where the very disciplined milk cows were lined up at the door from the corral. Even the order of the cows was well established and seldom, if ever, wavered. (For those who aren't familiar with dairy cows, they are creatures of habit that like consistent routines.)

Before the cows were admitted, the lanterns were hung on their hooks, hay and a little grain were spread into the center-aisle bunks next to the stanchions. Each stanchion would accommodate eight milk cows and hold their heads secure while they ate their breakfasts and awaited their turns to be relieved of their heavy bags of milk.

The barn door would swing open and eight cows on each side would put their heads through the stanchions, which were then locked. Once secure, Everett, with the bucket of warm soapy water, would quickly clean the teats of each cow.

Boyd and the hired man would then each grab their short, crude, one-legged stool, a dairy bucket, and go to work. They milked from the right side of the cow, facing forward with the left side of their face pressed against the warm cow. Pleasant really, unless the cow was wet.

Every milker has his own set routine, but usually they work the back two teats first and when those two quarters are nearly dry, will shift to the front teats. When the flow of milk there slows down, he would strip the back teats dry, then strip the front teats. Total elapsed time about six to eight minutes, and the milker is left with a couple of gallons of warm, frothy milk, very strong forearm muscles and a firm grip.

The bucket of milk from each of the two milkers would then be handed off to Everett. He would head back into the night with his cargo destined for the separator room on the house porch.

Everett and Dee were both anxious to join the milking crew, but every time they brought up the subject, they got their answer in the form of a squirt of milk to the face. (Cats love this, boys do not.)

Separating Cream

After its thorough cleaning from the last milking, Gertie and the girls would have the separator re-assembled and ready to go. Everett would pour both buckets into the top container, position a bucket under the skim milk spout and a smaller bucket under the cream spout.

He would then start turning the manual crank. The centrifugal force in the device efficiently separated the cream from the whole milk, leaving a container of rich cream and another of skim milk.

Chapter 7: A Day in the Life of the Last Dollar Ranch—Circa 1935

This milking/separating routine was repeated until all the cows, the number varying depending on the season from 30 to 45 total, were milked dry and turned out to feed and drink. The milking operation would be repeated again at precisely 4 p.m. every afternoon.

The precious, rich cream would be poured into a 10-gallon, 23-inch-high, metal cream can. When it was filled, it would be lowered into the hand-dug well near the house and suspended with ropes to partially submerge the can in the water which would keep it from freezing.

Later, when the Collins had eight full cream cans, either Everett or Dee would saddle up a horse, then fix the halters and pack saddles on two draft horses. They had made four custom panniers out of scrap metal. Each pannier held two cream cans.

From his saddle horse, one of the boys would lead the two pack animals through the snow to the county road, then another mile to the small narrow gauge railroad siding and store at Noel, which had daily rail service to and from Ridgway and Telluride. The clerk would help him with the cream cans, placing them on a platform where the train engineer would stop the box car.

Most of the cream would go to the Ridgway store and creamery where a clerk would record the cream shipment into a ledger with the amount and agreed unit price indicated. The cream was frequently accompanied by a list of goods the Collins' wanted on the next train to Noel. The order would be reliably handled initially by the train conductor and would contain a list of staples (flour, sugar, coffee, etc.) as well as such items as yards of cloth, tools, ammunition, etc. The order would be filled by a clerk at the store with the goods then placed in a box for delivery. The priced items were entered in the store ledger with the cost deducted from the credit available from the cream sale.

The cream sent to Telluride would fetch a premium price because of the relative demand and prosperity of the miners. This was usually a cash transaction.

By 7 a.m., the milking and separating chores were complete. It was getting light and time for breakfast. The men were hungry and the girls in the kitchen weren't going to disappoint. With the cold, physically demanding work, a large hot breakfast was needed to replenish the body for the daylight chores. The menu only varied slightly from day to day and would consist of:

- *strong black coffee*
- *cold whole milk*
- *biscuits (baked minutes before)*
- *an ample bowl of sausage gravy*
- *warm oatmeal*
- *a separate platter of ham, bacon or sausage*
- *an iron skillet of scrambled eggs (it was not the done thing to request eggs over easy)*
- *pancakes with blackstrap cane molasses syrup which arrived regularly from the store in Ridgway*

Once breakfast was over, the men could rightfully call themselves "satisfied." It was then time to tackle the day's chores. Every one of the men, old and young, had their specific chores to get done.

Morning Chores

The hired man would, as it has been known for generations, "slop the hogs." In the hog shed were two large boars (males) in a separate pen; five, full-grown sows (breeding females) and an assortment of some 15 piglets of varying sizes.

Grain, either oats, barley or wheat (whatever was most available), had been put into a small barrel the evening before and left to soak in skim milk overnight. The contents of the barrel were poured into troughs along with the "slop bucket" from the kitchen (think vegetable peels, leftover food scraps, etc.). Additional buckets of skim milk were added. Yes, this was indeed "sloppy!"

After the hogs were fed, the hired man would take buckets of skim milk to the calves in their barn where they could drink their fill directly from the buckets. Some hay from the loft would be tossed down in the small mangers for the calves.

Boyd would feed the horses hay in their corral while checking each of the four mules, two saddle horses, and some 15 versatile draft horses. Foals were raised on the ranch from a Percheron stud (male) he had named "Midnight," and a saddle horse mare (female). He was very proud of his horses and wanted them well conditioned for the work they performed throughout the year.

Once Boyd had fed his selected team, the boys and the hired man would harness them and hook them onto a large hay sled. They would then travel to the nearest stack of hay and pull along side. Two would climb on the stack with their pitchforks and one would stay on the sled to level the hay coming down.

When the sled was completely loaded with hay, it was pulled to the milk cows and the hay spread on clean snow. Then it was reloaded with hay and taken to the pregnant cows who would calve in a couple of months. The range cows would be fed next, with the third, sometimes the fourth, sled of hay.

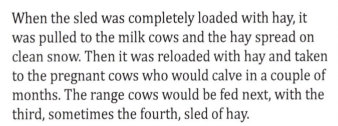

Finally, in a separate pasture were the three Holstein bulls (for the milk cows) and two Hereford bulls (for the range cows). Special care was given to the bulls for on 15 June they would be turned out with the ladies to do their very important, but taxing, service to insure a good calf crop the following April.

Once the cattle were fed, the crew would return to the homestead, drop the hay sled and hook onto a sled with a low, flat bed and sideboards about 12 inches high. This would be used daily to haul the manure from the cow barn, then the horse barn, and once a week, from the calf barn. The punishment for not doing this daily was to chip away the frozen manure the next day.

Once loaded, the man on the lines would guide the team to a grain field where the two men on the sled would feverishly scatter the manure while the team continued walking.

Dinner time!

This work would take them until noon, time for dinner, the main meal of the day. The men would wash up with warm water in a basin set up on the porch by Fern and Grace, shed their coats and boots, then sit at their designated places at the dining room table. This day the menu included:

- *black coffee*
- *cold whole milk*
- *homemade bread*

- *a pot roast in a large Dutch oven with beef from a steer butchered last fall, canned string beans from their summer garden, and potatoes from the same garden*

- *dessert would follow—this day, bread pudding*

It was now 12:30 p.m. and, while the girls cleared the table and did the dishes, the men would lie down flat on the dining room floor, sans pillows, for a power nap. When the mantel clock struck one, the nap was over. It was time to go back to work. They had three hours to get special chores done before milking time.

Afternoon Chores

The hired man, who possessed some basic blacksmithing skills, would light his small forge in the tool shed. His job on this day was to forge three sturdy strap hinges for a heavy new gate they wanted to build next to the horse barn.

With the forge heating, he found the broken four-foot wagon wheel he had set aside to provide the material he needed for his hinges. With broken wooden spokes, it was easy to remove the worn iron rim, which he cut into three equal pieces with a hacksaw.

Back in the tool shed, he would heat and straighten the tire iron sections using a heavy anvil and a 2½-pound hammer. Once straight, he would then forge a round eye on one end, then, with a standing hand-operated drill, would drill holes for the long lag screws to fasten the hinge to the horizontal gate poles.

Tomorrow he would forge the three vertical pins, which would be attached to a heavy cedar gate post. These pins would receive the strap hinges.

Boyd, with help from Dee and Everett, would spend some time repairing harness with harness leather obtained from the tannery in Montrose (ordered through the Ridgway store).

He worked with the boys for the first hour, showing them, once again, how to use the awl (leather punch) without punching a hole in their hand, make the hole pattern and, finally, how to sew it with the heavy thread covered with beeswax from a handy block.

> By 8 p.m. no one needs to be reminded it was bedtime. Tomorrow would be another long day— short only of daylight.

Once he was satisfied with the boys' work on the harness, Boyd selected one team to have their shoes removed, their hoofs trimmed and their winter shoes reset. These shoes are special as they prevent slipping with ¾" heel calks on the shoes for the hind legs and ½" toe calks for the front legs.

At 3:45 p.m., all hands put their tools away and headed for the separator room to pick up their buckets for the 4 p.m. milking. By 7 p.m., the evening milking chore was complete, it was dark again, and the men headed to the house.

Gathering Eggs

Each morning, one of the girls would make a trip to the chicken coop to gather what the hens had produced. During the afternoon in the house, Fern and Grace had been making simple sundresses for summer from patterned flour sacks on the Singer treadle sewing machine before setting the table for supper. The following day, with yet more flour sacks, they would make pillowcases and tea towels.

Supper was a light meal—sometimes bread and soup. Tonight it is a light stew with meat and vegetables left over from the pot roast dinner.

By 8 p.m. no one needs to be reminded it was bedtime. Tomorrow would be another long day— short only of daylight.

Summer

When: Friday, 16 August 1935

Where: The Collins Place on the top of Dallas Divide, elevation 9,300'

The temperature would be mid-40s at night and up to the 80s during the day. The sun would first hit the homestead at 5:32 a.m. (no daylight savings time in those days) and go down over the west ridge at 6:58 p.m.

These were long days, which were welcome, for there was much to be done every day before and after the sun shone.

The ranch was simply beautiful; the meadows were covered with wildflowers and the peaks still showing signs of the last of their snow. There was one constant at the Collins Place, regardless of the season, and that was starting the milking chore at 4 a.m. This day, of course, was no exception. The three-man milking and separating crew would not change, except, sometimes, in composition.

But this early summer morning was markedly different from the winter setting— there were more people to work and feed. The family of Boyd and Gertie, their boys (Dee and Everett), and the girls (Fern and Grace), were augmented with two young girls who were staying in the lower bedroom ready to assist with the household chores and to tend to Gertie's large garden.

The small bunkhouse also housed a second hired man who slept in the spare bunk. The dining room table seats were all spoken for; so another small table for four was squeezed into the room to accommodate the overload.

As Gertie and Boyd rolled out of their beds at 3:45 a.m. to stoke the fires and remove the morning chill, the house (and outhouse) became a beehive of activity.

The milking crew left to complete its task much the same as in the winter, but with more cows to milk and less hay to throw in the bunks. The cream produced was easier to transport in their 1917 Dodge truck to the railhead at Noel.

Everyone else quickly moved on to their assigned chores, some inside getting breakfast started and some outside.

A hearty breakfast was consumed, a bit more hurried now for there was much to be accomplished.

By mid-August some 20 acres of winter wheat had been cut with a binder and the bundles stacked in neat shocks which would preserve the grain until the threshing machine and custom crew would arrive at the ranch late next month.

Volume 4: The Golden Years

Above: McCormick-Deering binder and left, steel-wheeled tractor

The fields of barley and oats were maturing. In a week or so the men would hitch a team to the binder, which they had purchased some 20 years earlier.

By this time, they had a fairly reliable steel-wheeled McCormick-Deering tractor, but they preferred to use horses on all the fieldwork except spring plowing.

The most important daily chore during the summer was the time-consuming task of irrigating with the precious water distributed to the grain fields and hay meadows—this was essential for the Collins very livelihood. One, and often times, two men would spend their entire day tending to the head gate at Leopard Creek and the two miles of ditch that transported the water to the fields. Then, using canvas dam "sets," the water would flow into smaller, secondary ditches to flood, by gravity, the various fields thereby watering the crops.

It was, and remains to the present day, an essential task to be performed by a skilled, hardworking person with a keen eye for nature's contours. Of course, sometimes you had to wait for the water, so, out of sight of the others, they could take time out to record their labor on the aspen trees.

Once the hogs were fed, the horses tended to, eggs gathered and chickens fed, including the chicks ordered through the Ridgway store in April (which were by this time plump little pullets), and the range cows moved to a fresh pasture, the day's work began.

During the summer, the cow barn was only cleaned every second day since there was no fear of freezing. Instead of the sled used to carry the manure to the fields in the winter, in the summer this chore was performed with a new-fangled John Deere manure spreader and a team.

Gardening Chores

For Gertie and the girls residing on the Collins Place, one of the most demanding and rewarding tasks was in the vegetable garden. Their large garden was located about 300 yards north of the homestead, just off the entrance road and alongside the Eagle Ditch, which bisects the ranch to deliver water across the

Manure spreader

county road to the neighbors' hay meadows. The Collins did not own any water rights from the ditch, but by law, it could be used to water livestock, and no one would argue that watering a garden from the ditch wasn't okay.

Earlier in the summer, the men tilled the sizable garden with a shallow plow then went over it with a horse-drawn harrow to prepare a soft seedbed in the black, fertile soil. They also built a woven wire fence on the perimeter to keep out the rabbits and other hungry small animals.

At this altitude, over 9,000', the growing season was short, but with timely skilled preparation, seeding, watering and weeding, the garden would produce a real bounty of root vegetables. Tomatoes and other above-ground vegetables were simply not viable, but string beans and pinto beans did well. On the other hand, beets, carrots, onions, parsnips, radishes, garlic, turnips, horseradish and—the most important—potatoes grew large and in great abundance. Cabbage, to make the very popular sauerkraut in five-gallon crocks, was also prized. And, as a cool-season crop, it grew well in this climate.

This day was vegetable-canning day. After pulling and digging the vegetables, the girls would bring their harvest to the house to be cleaned, cut, cooked and placed in one-quart mason jars that would be sealed, then placed in a "pressure canner" for final sealing and preservation.

The contents would then be served on the table during the cold months ahead, while the fresh vegetables were on the menu of every dinner and supper during these very active summer months.

Sickle mower

Side delivery rake

Haying

The men, meanwhile, were gearing up just after breakfast for another day in the hay fields. The process was to cut the rich alpine grass when the seeds were in the dough stage with the nutritious leaves at full growth. Two teams, each pulling a John Deere #8 sickle mower, were continually circling the hay field to cut and lay down the grass. There it would lie for about four days of sunshine to dry but yet retain its nutrients (not unlike a dried apricot).

Once dry, the hay would be ready for stacking unless it had rained, in which case a horse drawn side-delivery rake would roll the grass over to let the moisture evaporate.

Buck rake

The next operation was to consolidate the hay into long, relatively straight windrows. The equipment for this task was a simple John Deere "dump rake" pulled by two fit horses that could travel all day at a slow, steady trot.

Once the windrows were formed, a "buck rake" with a long-toothed rake in front (sometimes called a "Go Devil"), pushed by a two-horse team, would gather a load of hay and deliver it to the "overshot stacker."

Go Devil (pushed instead of pulled)

Chapter 7: A Day in the Life of the Last Dollar Ranch—Circa 1935

Overshot stacker

This is a photo of the Collins stacking operation. The teams in front of the stack were on buck rakes. A single man is on the stack. The man on the left is leading the stacker horse.

The hay from the front of the dump rake would be deposited on the forks of the stacker. When it was full, a man with a single horse would pull on a cable with a pulley system designed to lift the hay high overhead to a point past vertical. Then the hay would slide off the rake and land on top of the stack.

Two men would work on the stack with pitchforks to keep the sides of the stack high and straight. If the two men on the stack were working hard with their backs to the stacker, the man on the ground might slowly and quietly lift the next load of hay and dump it on the unsuspecting stackers. All but two men would have a great laugh.

Hay rack

Besides putting the hay into long stacks, loose hay would also be delivered to the "hay mounts" or "lofts" in the various barns with a hay wagon.

That is a brief description of the haying operation, which would continue for several weeks, seven days a week, with rain providing the only break.

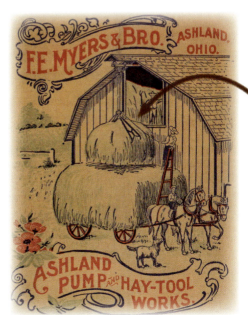

Hay grapple

Butchering Days

Tomorrow, Saturday, was time for another chore that would require two men and all the ladies. A neighbor would help, arriving with two hogs to be butchered. The Collins would add two hogs of their own, each weighing around 200-300 pounds. A sturdy frame with a sliding block-and-tackle had been built for the butchering chores. Today it was hogs; in a few weeks, it would be several yearling calves.

The hogs, pulled one at a time by their back legs, would be positioned under the frame, then would be lifted, by their back legs, up so their head was about two feet off the ground. Once all four were hanging, a man with a very sharp knife would cut their jugular veins and the blood would gush forth. This operation is the origin of the old saying "bleeding like a stuck pig." In a matter of a few minutes, the hogs would be deceased and completely bled out.

The next operation was to dip the hogs, one at a time, into a suitably-sized metal tank full of scalding hot water, for only about a minute. This would clean and soften the hair, which was then removed by large scalping knives, sometimes a sharp woodworking drawknife.

Once the hair was removed, the animal would be skinned, with the skin cut into long strips to be cooked with pork and served as very tasty "cracklins," what are commonly known today as pork rinds, or in Spanish, "chicharrón."

The hogs would be gutted and cut into quarters with the fat removed and cooked (rendered), to recover the liquid as lard. To a portion of the lard, lye with honey or lavender powder (from lavender bushes) would be added to make soap for hands and body as well as for washing clothes. In the soap-making process, Fern and Grace would add, for themselves and their mother's exclusive use, crushed wild rose petals (from wild rose bushes) to give some of the bars color and fragrance.

The neighbors eventually left in their wagon with eight quarters of pork and an ample supply of lard and soap. The Collins crew would retain the by-products and perhaps four quarters, with the remainder going to the railhead at Noel for delivery to meat markets in Ridgway or Telluride. The Collins had built a small, but efficient, smoke house to cure the ham and bacon.

Also on the schedule for Saturday would be catching and cleaning eight plump pullets, which would be the savory entrée for the haying crew's Sunday dinner.

Each year, Boyd and Gertie would have raised more than 120 "free-range" chickens, which they ordered as hatchlings through the store in Ridgway. This type of prep work for the dinner table was common to all farms and ranches during the depression years.

One of the boys would be armed with a long pole outfitted with a wire hook fixed to the end. Spotting a suitable candidate, the kid would hook the chicken by one leg, then hold it upside down by both legs and deliver it to Boyd, the adult executioner at the chopping block, which was most often used to split wood for the stove. Two long nails had been driven partially into the block to form a "V" with the nails about one inch apart at the base. Boyd would place the chicken's head into the "V," legs were then pulled to stretch the neck out, and with the axe handy, deliver a smart blow on the neck and the chicken's life was over. Bleeding profusely, the chicken was placed on very wobbly legs to bleed out—hopefully near no one.

The next step was to submerse the now-deceased chicken into a bucket of scalding water. Experience would dictate just how many seconds this would take—too long and the skin would weaken and tear with the plucking; too short and the feathers wouldn't give up their hold. If the pinfeathers were hard to pick, the plucker would need to perfect the scalding operation. Properly performed, the chicken could be plucked clean of all feathers in a couple of minutes. Once all the pinfeathers were removed, the chicken would be passed to an adult for removal of the innards.

The cleaned chicken would then be placed in a bucket of cold water where it would remain until just before dinner on Sunday when, in the kitchen, the feet were removed and the chicken cut in the traditional pieces.

Wash day at Last Dollar

The final step was to place the pieces into a paper sack containing flour, a little salt and some pepper, shake the bag to get the flour covering on each piece, then carefully arrange the pieces in a hot iron skillet. The resulting fried chicken was a delicious and memorable feast.

When Monday rolled around, it was, by tradition in all rural homes, wash day. All the ladies would take part in this hours-long chore.

Collins boys helping stack hay bundles down on the rocks.

Grain threshing operation and machinery

Grain Threshing

All this summer activity would culminate in September. With the oats, barley and wheat cut, bundled and stacked in shocks in the field, a custom threshing crew would arrive on schedule with their iron-wheeled tractor equipped with a power take-off pulley on the side and a large belt-powered threshing machine.

The traveling crew would operate the tractor and threshing machine while it was the responsibility of the homesteader to pick up the bundles from the field with teams and hay wagons and deliver the bundles next to the feed chute and drag chain on the machine. The bundles would be pitched on the chain drive one at a time from wagons on both sides.

It was also the responsibility of the landowner to collect the clean grain from the machine, haul it in a grain wagon to the granary where separate bins, with every effort made to keep out mice during the winter, would store the grain until it was needed for the livestock and chickens. It also could be collected in gunnysacks (also known as burlap bags) at the threshing machines if it was to be sold through the Ridgway store.

The week of threshing was the most intensive activity of the year and, when complete, marked the end of the summer season.

Author's Note:

Hopefully, with these descriptions, the reader will have gained some appreciation of these tough, hardy people who were indeed good at what they did in their effort to make a better life for themselves and their children. While we have gained much in the way of technology and creature comforts, we have also lost many of the lessons our forefathers (and mothers) knew well. For example, they couldn't just run down to the grocery store and pick up what they wanted; rather they had to know how to produce their own food. The John Deere repairman didn't make farm visits, so they needed to learn enough about how machines worked to repair their own.

Today, most Americans are not very self-sufficient. As we've specialized and each person knows more and more about less and less, we've lost some of our common sense and self-reliance. We could benefit from more of the "pioneer kind" in our modern age.

The Sister Ranch—Centennial

It was 1989 when we acquired Last Dollar, and the next two years were devoted to preserving the land and restoring the house and log outbuildings. During that short period it became abundantly clear that, at that altitude (9,300') with the normal heavy snowfall, this was no place to winter cattle.

A search began for a ranch within reasonable proximity at a lower elevation with sufficient hay production to enable our goal of having a modest cow/calf operation. Duane and I again made contact with Nancy Bradburn, our respected real estate agent for Last Dollar. Our timing was fortunate for not only were ranch prices depressed, but also she had a listing that could suit our needs.

The ranch, north of Ridgway and some 20 road miles from Last Dollar, was a full half-mile lower in elevation and about the same size—392 acres with nearly 100 acres irrigated. In addition, there was a bonus. One-half mile of the beautiful Uncompahgre River flowed through the ranch!

This particular piece of real estate had been homesteaded by the pioneering James Nelson Smith family in 1879. At that time, this was Ute Indian territory. Fast forward 110 years and the fifth generation of Smiths owned and worked the place. After a lifetime of hard work with few monetary rewards, brothers Jim, Verle and Rollen were ready to cash out and retire.

The Smiths also owned several thousand acres of high country, just 10 miles west as the crow flies on the eastern slope of Horsefly Peak. This alpine pasture would be held by the brothers to be passed on to their heirs. If this could be leased for summer grazing, it would be an ideal setup.

A unique connection

There was also a unique connection between my family and the Smiths. In the 1960s, Jim—the eldest brother—decided to supplement the Smith family income by becoming a Colorado brand inspector. He was posted to Julesburg where my father was a respected cattleman.

Jim Smith was called to Dad's feedlot whenever Dad received or shipped cattle, as well as when he bought calves to pasture during the summer before trucking them to the feedlot. Over the years, they developed a great deal of mutual respect. During several years in the 1960s, my father bought all the calves from the Smith's Ouray County ranch—sight unseen. The transaction was based solely on Jim Smith's assurance of quality and at an agreed price. The result was beneficial for both parties and was sealed with a handshake, a stronger commitment to those men than any written contract.

Hence, for decades there existed a relationship between the Smiths and the Kontnys—a bond I inherited. That, in essence, was an advantage I enjoyed over other prospective buyers when Nancy introduced Duane and me to the three Smith brothers in the kitchen of Rollen's house on the ranch.

Duane and I were satisfied that the "Smith place" would ideally satisfy our needs for hay production and provide a good environment for winter feeding and spring calving. The price they were asking was also reasonable, in line with the then-current market.

Rollen, Verle and Jim Smith

> I stood up and asked if it was acceptable. Jim stood and extended his hand. Verle and Rollen did likewise. We shook hands and the deal was done.

Discussing the deal

We sat around the kitchen table for more than an hour with Jim Smith relating story after story of his long, positive association with my father during his tenure in the Julesburg community. Nancy was quiet and patient, with a copy of our simple, compliant offer ready for signature in her briefcase. Finally, I asked Nancy to table a copy for each of the brothers to read, which they briefly scanned.

Then, I stood up and asked if it was acceptable. Jim stood and extended his hand. Verle and Rollen did likewise. We shook hands and the deal was done. They asked for a few days to review the offer with their lawyer, which was immediately agreed to with the understanding that any wording that needed changing would be addressed before signing. It was indisputable in the minds of everyone; they had sold and we had bought the ranch.

Within a few days, we did indeed sign the real estate papers, and then Duane and I walked with Jim and Rollen down to the equipment shed and agreed on the price of every piece of equipment proposed for sale by Jim and Rollen. It could not have been a cleaner nor more pleasant transaction.

While we now owned an ideal property for our purposes, it did indeed require a great deal of effort to transform it into our vision of a good working ranch. Not, mind you, as substantial an effort as that which was required at Last Dollar, but a great deal of work, nonetheless.

The Smiths were not prepared to sell their high country land, which we would need for summer grazing if we were to avoid leasing government-owned grazing rights, which could be an operational headache. They offered us a right of first refusal to purchase some 1,600 acres they owned, which suited our needs, as well as a long-term summer grazing lease agreement.

The ranch is located nearly equidistant (12 miles) between the small towns of Ridgway (to the south) and prosperous Montrose (to the north). Montrose serves a greater population of some 40,000 people with all the attendant amenities, including an excellent two-runway airport with flights to various cities.

Volume 4: The Golden Years

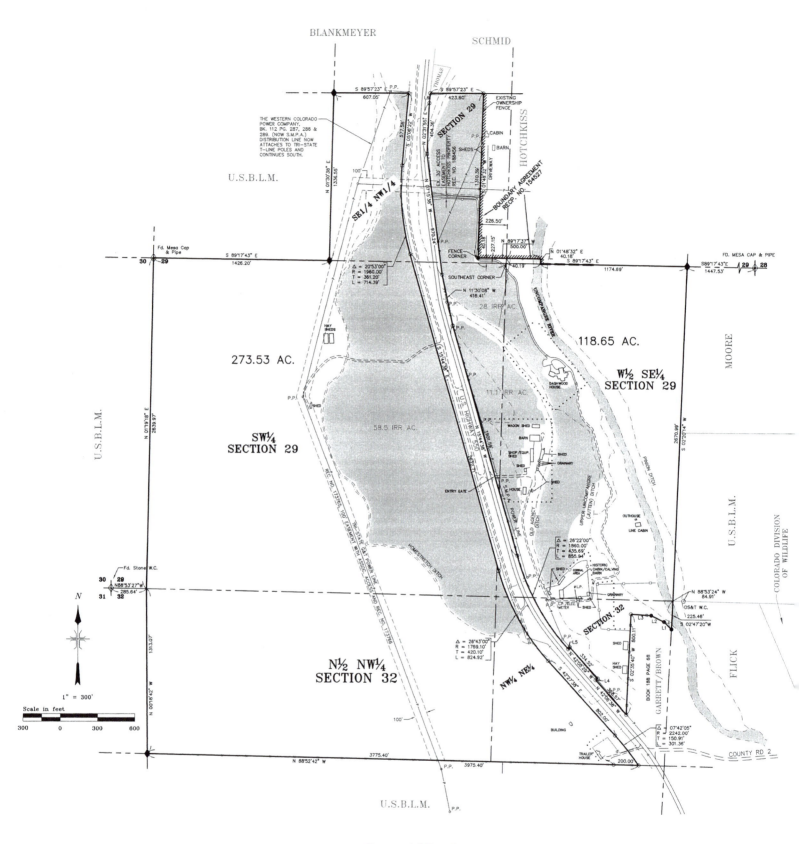

Centennial Ranch

The ranch had excellent historic water rights sufficient to cover the irrigated acreage. The property sits in a narrow canyon of the north-flowing Uncompahgre River with the eastern and western boundaries stretching from rim to rim. The river runs a half-mile through the ranch with no public access. The Uncompahgre is known as a "tailwater" river since it is just some three miles downstream from the Ridgway Reservoir—completed in 1987 and filled in 1990—thus assuring a regulated flow of water.

State Highway 550 bisects the ranch and is the only paved access road from Montrose to all points south. Therefore, the two lanes carry a considerable amount of traffic. Also, because the ranch covers the entire valley floor, it has, for more than a century, provided easement access to the narrow-gauge railway (abandoned in 1952), telephone and power lines, water lines and four irrigation ditches servicing fields to the north.

Some 120 acres of the ranch were in the original river flood plain east of the highway with about 270 acres west of the paved road at a slightly higher elevation. The ranch borders government land to the east, west and, except for small holdings along the river, to the north and south as well.

Hay fields in the valley had been developed in the early days whenever irrigation water was available. The generations of Smiths had been cattlemen, so few crops were ever planted except those that supported livestock.

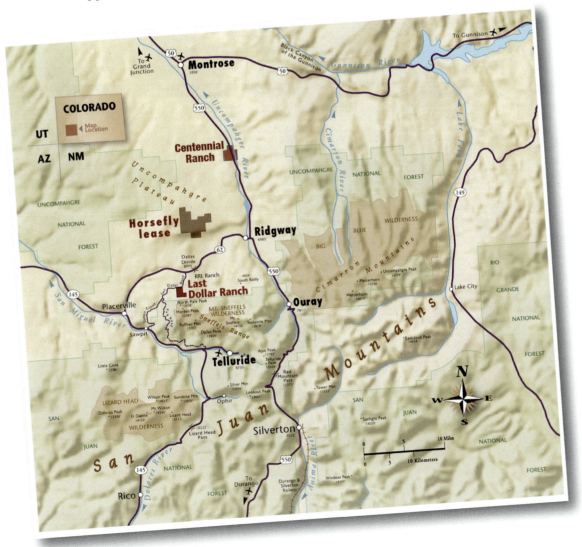

Existing improvements

The house occupied by Rollen Smith and his wife, Alyce Mae, was built circa 1950. It was a Montgomery Ward "kit house," ordered through their catalog with detailed instructions for placing the concrete foundations—and in this case, a ¾ basement.

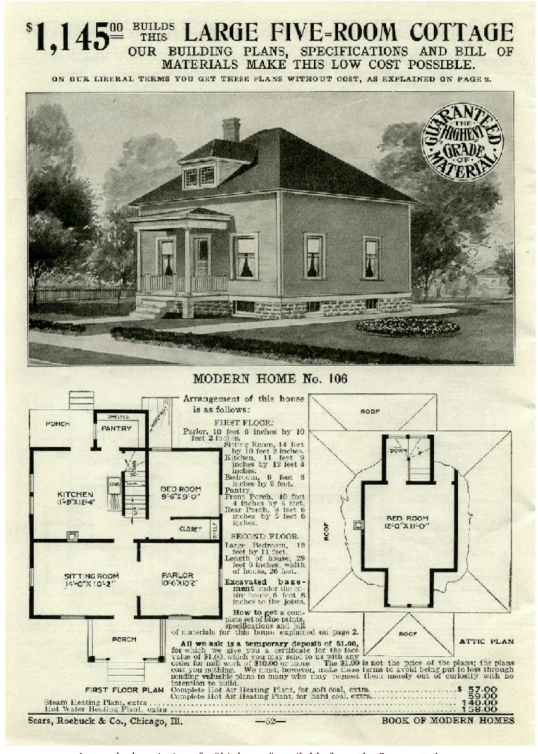

A sample description of a "kit house" available from the Sears catalog.

Chapter 8: The Sister Ranch – Centennial

The original Smith log cabin (now a calving shed) where they raised their family of nine children.

Once the prep work was completed by the Smiths, the bill of materials for the three-bedroom house was loaded in a box car by *Montgomery Ward* and dispatched to the small siding of Eldridge near the house site. The box car contained detailed instructions for construction by the Smiths, pre-cut floor and structural lumber, flooring, siding, roofing, windows, doors, electrical and plumbing fixtures, et. al. Really, it was a complete package that could easily be erected with limited building experience.

The original log cabin, constructed adjacent to the river just a year after the Smith's arrival, had been moved to higher ground a quarter of a mile away in the 1930s to escape the periodic floods of the river caused by heavy rains anywhere in its extensive drainage area to the south.

Duane and I later pried open the door of this cabin and found the interior stacked to the ceiling with old harness, discarded furniture and great quantities of dust-covered junk. It was several months before we discovered that this cabin, with its board-and-batten siding and lath-and-plaster interior was, in fact, a log cabin.

Women of the day did not like to be known as living in a log cabin, the ultimate example of low-cost housing of the day. So, as soon as funds and time were available, the men would crudely flatten the exterior of the logs with an adze, then cover them with rough-cut board-and-batten. The interior faces of the logs were also given the adze treatment, then lath and plaster applied. The result was an attractive cabin with thick walls that provided excellent insulation.

> The biggest project we had to face, however, was the removal of more than a century's accumulation of pure junk.

Restoring the ranch

The perimeter barbed-wire fences, as well as the interior cross fences, were in sorry shape. Each spring a man would walk the fence, patching it as necessary to hold livestock for another season. Likewise, the board corrals had deteriorated over the years as had the livestock shelter sheds within the pens.

There were no hay sheds. Since the first hay was put up on the ranch, it had been stacked loose or in small bales wherever it would be handy for winter feeding. In the later decades, these stacks would be temporarily covered in plastic tarps, which were held in place with hundreds of discarded tires.

The biggest challenge was to reclaim the old flood plain in the river bottom. The original course of the river wound around the bottom, mostly at some 100-200 feet from the sandstone cliffs to the east. This was a problem for the Smiths since the land between the river and the cliffs was not accessible and tempted cows with calves to cross the river to seek fresh grass.

This was solved circa 1935 when the Smiths bought a dozer to move the stream to the east, immediately adjacent to the cliffs, where it remains to the current day. One could do things in those times regarding river issues that current regulations and the Army Corps of Engineers would never consider.

The biggest project we had to face, however, was the removal of more than a century's accumulation of pure junk. Rotting piles of hay, abandoned small buildings, discarded equipment, stacks of old fence posts and wire, and the daily trash that tends to pile up when there is no one willing to pick it up were scattered everywhere.

At the shops and equipment shed in those days, when one needed to add a can of oil to a tractor, the empty container was simply tossed over the edge of the yard and into the bushes and weeds of the ditch bank. Out of sight, out of mind.

Another of the restoration challenges was to clean up the tangle of fallen cottonwood trees in the river bottom—an accumulation of a century of stumps, weeds, rotting trunks and branches. I have often said I didn't think a garter snake could get through that mess.

The cleanup would begin like the first bite of a second elephant. It would eventually take us 11 years, working with our own limited manpower and equipment, to get the ranch in the pristine condition it enjoys currently.

A Brief History of Centennial

Author's Note:

Not unlike our decision at Last Dollar, one of our early priorities after we purchased Centennial in 1992 was to document its rich history. So, again, we commissioned local genealogy writer, Dona Freeman, to research, then document, the history of the Smith Ranch.

Dona approached the assignment with her usual dedication and vigor, collecting the photos and happenings of the Smith family over the five generations that owned and worked the ranch for more than a century.

In this chapter, I gratefully draw from Dona's book, Smith Ranch, Colona, Colorado 1879-1992, *published in 1992.*

According to local lore, James and Charlotte Smith loaded their three young children and all their worldly possessions in a large mule-drawn wagon and made the trek over the Continental Divide from Alamosa to western Colorado in 1879. They trailed about a dozen head of cattle, determined to start a new life as ranchers supplying meat to the hungry miners in Ouray and Telluride.

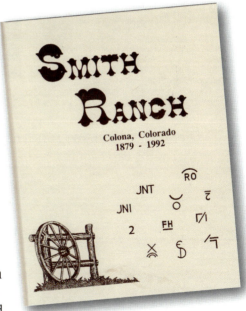

When they reached the Uncompahgre[1] River, where Montrose is now located, they turned south and followed it upstream 12 miles into a beautiful mountain valley. The valley (in Indian Territory) was home to the friendly Ute tribe. The Smiths traded two beeves in exchange for permission to build a log home next to the river and graze their cattle on the rich grass at the bottom of a narrow canyon.

Two years later, the U.S. government broke its treaty with the Utes, pushing the tribe out of its ancestral home into the harsh desert of Utah to the west. The Smith family stayed and eventually acquired 392 acres along the Uncompahgre through the Homestead Act. Working with neighbors, they dug a three-mile-long ditch to irrigate fields so they could grow winter feed for their livestock. They later added 3,000 acres of high-country summer grazing land to their holdings.

---

1 *"Uncompahgre" is a Ute word that, loosely translated, means warm, muddy water.*

> Life was hard, but they persevered, raising a large family in a log cabin that still stands.

JAMES NELSON SMITH is the patriarch of this Smith family that came here in 1879. He and his wife Charlotte Eldridge Smith raised eight of their nine children on the family ranch at Colona, and all but the first few were born at the ranch, with the older ones being born in the San Luis Valley. There were eventually five generations of the Smith family that lived on the home ranch over 100 years after 1879 until the ranch was sold in 1992.

Life was hard, but they persevered, raising a large family in a log cabin that still stands. This is a brief of the early Smiths.

When they arrived, the Smiths were not the only whites in the Uncompahgre Valley. The government, fearing trouble with the Indians because of broken treaties and a heavy influx of prospectors and miners seeking their fortunes, established a "Cantonment on the Uncompahgre" in 1880. The camp was located just three miles north of what would become the Smith Place.

Chapter 9: A Brief History of Centennial

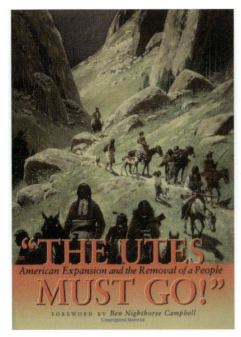

In 1881, after several incidents involving a few renegade Utes, the whites in the region indicated they had had enough of the Indians. A large, illustrated advertisement in the *Denver Tribune* blared, "The Utes Must Go." In a shameful chapter of our nation's history, the Utes in this beautiful valley, their homeland for centuries, had another treaty broken and all the Utes were relocated west to the desert lands of Utah.

The Smiths exercised what was referred to as "squatter's rights," in their log cabin next to the river. Their family flourished with six siblings being added to the three who had made the trek over the Continental Divide. During those early years, the Smiths were granted title through various Homestead Acts of Congress to the acreage in the valley as well as to several thousand acres in the high country to the west.

Their singular mission in those early years was to raise beef cattle. This focus on cattle would continue for all the generations that followed.

To prosper in the cattle business of that era, you first and foremost needed grass to feed the livestock in the summer and grass to be cut, dried and stacked for winter feed. Summer feed was best provided in the high country—above 8,000 feet in elevation—where the cows and their calves could thrive in the rich alpine grass.

The challenge for cattlemen was to raise and stack sufficient hay during the summer months to keep the livestock in good condition over the long, cold winter months. A rancher, therefore, needed sufficient flat acreage at an elevation lower than 7,000' (so that the growing season lasted long enough to produce the needed hay).

The key, then, was sufficient water to irrigate those fields. Hence, one of the earliest priorities for the Smith pioneers and their neighbors was to construct a ditch to carry water from the Uncompahgre River to their hay fields. Work on the ditch, identified as the "Home Stretch Ditch" in the 1884 Abstract, started immediately after the request was approved.

Building such a ditch, some three miles in length, was no easy task. Working with the other ditch shareholders, the Smiths would hitch their horse to a simple Fresno scraper and go to work building the ditch.

ABSTRACT 1884—HOME STRETCH DITCH— Location Certificate. Work commenced Mch. 1, 1884 - for ditch and irrigation purposes, and tapping waters of Uncompahgre River at a point which bears 73½ degrees West 900 feet from S.E. Corner of Sec. 32, Twp. 47, N. R. 8 W., N.M.P.M. (Recites courses and distances), and emptying into Uncompahgre River. 4 feet wide at bottom, 7 feet wide at top, 1½ feet deep. We claim 1500 cubic inches per second of water of said Uncompahgre River. Owners of said Ditch are:- Thos. Eldridge 30 shares, George Lee 15 shares, J.N. Smith 25 shares, Wm. Eggleston 15 shares, Asbury Armlin, 5 shares, James Kettle 25 shares, Velmer Paul, 10 shares, Adelia Brower 80 shares, the whole number of shares being 205.

With the Home Stretch Ditch completed and a reliable source of irrigation water established, the early Smiths concentrated on improving their cow herd and building the corrals, shelter sheds, feed bunks for the cows, shops, grain bins, equipment, et. al., needed to support their livestock.

Soon the annual activities settled into a well-rehearsed routine. Enabled by the fact that a cow's gestation period was about nine months, and the fact she would recycle within two months (meaning come back into estrus and be ready to breed again), the annual calendar varied little. The bulls would be turned out with the ladies on 15 May for calving to begin mid-February. The weeds and grass in the ditch would be burned as soon as the snow melted out of the ditch bottoms, usually in mid-April (this management practice was used to clean out the dead weeds that accumulated over the past season).

When the ditch was burned and ready to carry water, the long daily summer chore of irrigating the hay fields would begin. The cows were kept off the hay fields, and turned out on the dryland portion of the ranch to feed on the spring grass.

As soon as the snow melted on the Horsefly and Iron Springs properties, some 10 miles west, and both at elevations over 9,000', a three-day trek was organized to drive the cows with their calves to the upper pastures for the summer. Once the cows were out of the valley, the first of two cuttings of hay would commence.

The cows and their 500+-pound calves would return to the valley in late October. When the snow covered the fall pasture, feeding the cows from a horse-drawn hay wagon or sled would begin.

In November, the calves would be weaned with top-quality heifers (females) retained to build up the herd. The remaining heifers and steers were sold. That was the only significant payday for the year, and it did not come without a great deal of work.

This routine would continue for the decades the various Smith generations raised cattle. The players changed, but the game never did; it simply evolved with new equipment and a few failed experiments with cash crops, specifically sugar beets and potatoes.

The big development of the lower Uncompahgre Valley was construction of the Gunnison Tunnel, which started in 1905 and was completed in 1909. At the time, this 5.8-mile tunnel was the longest irrigation tunnel in the world, and it brought a large quantity of water from the Gunnison River into the vast number of dry acres around Montrose.

It was such a big reclamation project that no less than the President of the United States William H. Taft attended the 1909 ceremony to push the big button and start the flow of water through the tunnel. To this day, the tunnel provides irrigation water for 80,000+ acres of farmland in the Uncompahgre Valley, as well as domestic water for most of the valley's inhabitants.

PRESIDENT TAFT opening the Gunnison Tunnel, Lujane, Colorado, Sept. 23, 1909. President Taft was presented with the handsome electrical device with which the tunnel headgate was raised. This device consisted of a mahogany box in which was contained a gold bell about three inches high. A silver plate formed a second lid to the box when the first lid was raised and the weight of the bell when it was placed on the lid by the hand of the President depressed the plate on springs under it and made the electrical contact. The bell was made of 18 karat Colorado gold and was purchased at the Denver Mint. It is a marvel of workmanship and, while it is customary in such cases to mould the article, in this case, the manufacturer, in order to avoid any possibility of flaws, had the bell hand-forged. (Photo courtesy of Uncompahgre Valley Water Users Assn.)

The succeeding generations of Smiths developed superb cowboy skills, for all cow work was performed on horseback. They not only bred their own horses, but they also became astute traders.

The only way to doctor a sick cow or calf in the high country was to rope the critter from a horse, throw it to the ground while the horse kept the rope tight, then give it the necessary treatment. Once that was accomplished, the hand went on to inspect the rest of the herd.

Fences in the high country were either non-existent or in constant need of repair from the winter snows, wildlife and falling trees.

The younger Smiths and their neighbors attended the Colona School, just two miles north of their home in the tiny settlement of Colona. A pioneer valley settler, Richard Collin, had read the book, *Ramona*, and had enjoyed it so much he chose part of his name and part of the name *Ramona,* to come up with the name "Colona" for the settlement.

The Colona School students circa 1927

Ralph Smith, of the second generation of Smiths, was born in 1884.

Ralph Nelson Smith

Rose Books Smith

Chapter 9: A Brief History of Centennial

With his wife, Rose, Ralph had three sons: James (Jim) born in 1912; Verle, born circa 1914; and Rollen, the youngest, born circa 1920. Their only daughter, Louise, was born in 1919.

Rollen married Alyce Mae Soderquist at a double ceremony with her brother, Andrew Soderquist, in 1946, when Rollen returned from a three-year hitch in the Navy. He had served on the Aleutians and Okinawa.

Rollen and friends

James "Jim" Smith

Spring bounty

97

Jim Smith married Lorraine Gollihar of Montrose, also in 1946. Verle never married.

Jim, Lorraine and their daughter, DeAryl "Dee," born in 1947

Rollen and his daughter, Sharon, born in 1948

The early Smith house

Six-year-old Sharon with the cows

Rollen with his Farmall tractor

Chapter 9: A Brief History of Centennial

Wind damage to the sheds at the homestead.

Rollen and Alyce Mae receiving the Honorary State Farmer degree from the Colorado FFA Association in 1975.

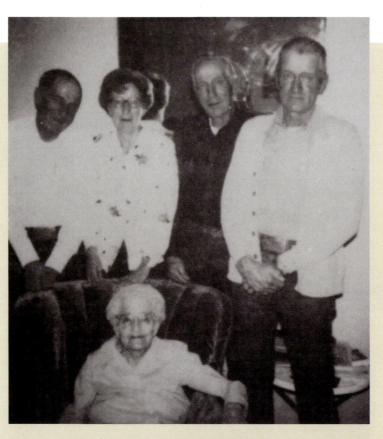

In October 1980, Rose Smith celebrated her 94th birthday with her four children; from left: Verle, Louise, Jim and Rollen. Rose died in 1985 at age 99.

Jim Smith

Verle Smith

Chapter 9: A Brief History of Centennial

> These people worked very hard, they played hard, were dedicated to their families, patriotic to their country and believed in God.

It was this recognition that inspired Joan and me to rename it "Centennial Ranch," when we purchased the property in 1992.

Lest the reader conclude that it was all work on this place during their century-long tenure as owner/operators, I would like to close this chapter on how these people and their neighbors had some good fun.

The venue for my story is the infamous Cow Creek Community Hall—just some six buggy miles from the ranch up the road along the river, across the Cow Creek bridge, then east on the creek road to a beautiful little valley. The community hall was built in 1936 to give the locals a place to congregate, celebrate and enjoy themselves.

I draw from a hard-back book publication of oral histories titled "Ranching History of Ouray County, Volume 1," printed in 2004. Everyone, young and old, from miles around came to these celebrations, usually held every month or two in the summer, but some in the dead of winter. The biggest bash was in April. The occasion? The Ouray County Cattlemen's Association annual dinner.

When they gathered in the early evening at the Community Hall, there was something for everyone. The ladies just loved to visit, sharing happenings and local gossip. Sometimes it was potluck, so they all brought piles of food, which they would serve at midnight. Little kids would play outside and, when they finally ran out of gas, would retire to the pile of coats in the cloakroom to fall asleep. The girls loved to dance to the music of the six-piece band made up of local ranch musicians.

What the band lacked in talent they made up for in enthusiasm, always with a heavy drum beat to keep the dancers in sync. The young men used the occasion to stretch their wings, usually with at least a pint bottle of whiskey hidden in the weeds. Once fired up, there always presented itself an opportunity for a good fight. The men simply talked and drank!

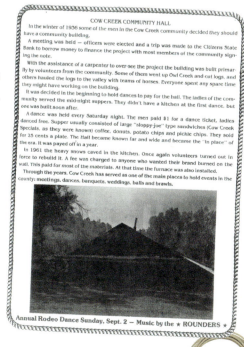

Annual Rodeo Dance Sunday, Sept. 2 — Music by the ★ ROUNDERS ★

101

From the interview of Arthur Dougherty:
"In the old days, the fights were different than they are now. If two guys decided they needed to fight, they would all leave the hall. All the friends would stand around and watch. The two fighters would go at it and just knock the shit out of each other. If one guy got knocked down, the other guy would help him up. They would fight until one had had enough. Then it was over! They would go have a drink together."

From the interview of Katherine Morris Gatschet:
"There were always lots of dances. We had dances at school and at the Cow Creek Community Hall. I always had my card full. (The girls had dance cards. When a man wanted to dance with a lady, he would ask her. The lady would write his name on her dance card. Then the lady would dance with the men in the order their names were on the card.)

"Vaughn Stealey was a great dancer. He taught me to waltz, varsouvienne (think "Put your little foot..."), and to two-step. He had the patience of Job!

"Different groups of women would take turns serving the meal at midnight. Everyone on the creek chipped in to help put on the dances.

"My father got drunk one time and crawled under the community hall. Then, he couldn't find his way back out. My mother was ready to kill him! Dad always had fun when he went out like that!"

Those were the days, when, "Dad always had fun when he went out like that!"

These people worked very hard, they played hard, were dedicated to their families, patriotic to their country and believed in God. I miss them!

Saving Centennial

Having acquired the Centennial Ranch, which was the ideal compliment to the Last Dollar Ranch for our purposes of creating a cow/calf operation, it was now time to go to work to ensure it satisfied its potential. The clean up was simple enough, but a monumental task. Nonetheless, we could handle it with our own small workforce. We worked for the next 11 years on that effort.

For the inspiration, design and construction of the desired new structures, I turned once again to the extraordinarily talented trio of Ted Moews (see *Dedication*), Howard McCall (*Dedication* of our *Heritage in Iron* book) and Duane Beamer (see *Dedication*). Here is how we went about creating what is today's Centennial Ranch.

Hay Fields

The first priority was to address any tasks needed to ensure maximum production of hay during the summer months for the cows and horses. The three-mile-long Home Stretch Ditch, which delivered our irrigation water, was in relatively good shape even though it was well over a century old. The Smiths had purchased plastic gated pipe to distribute the water from the ditch to the fields. Likewise, the hay fields had been maintained well, with only minor work required to obtain the optimum tonnage yield.

Fences and Corrals

Not surprisingly, all the barbed wire fencing, having served its useful life, was in serious need of replacement. Most of our fencing requirements were along the highway and at the north and south ends of the property. The steep slopes below the cliffs on the east and west boundaries were sufficient to keep livestock from wandering off in those directions.

To replicate historical fencing, we used two cedar posts set on eight-foot centers with four overlapping 16-foot poles securely fixed to the posts. The very hard cedar, available locally, has proven to resist rot for decades and has been the preferred material for posts ever since the first barbed wire was strung over the open range in the late 1800s.

Although it was a real challenge to dig deep postholes in the river bottom gravel, Chuck Cordova, our worm-fence contractor at Last Dollar, persevered and produced a sturdy, old-time scenic fence that will last decades.

The corrals where we would feed and work the cattle also needed replacing. The Smiths had designed a very workable set of corrals, so we elected to maintain the layout, but use stout salvaged railroad ties for the posts on 8-foot centers with five-high 2" x 6" boards lagged to the ties. They are as sturdy as any corrals ever built, adequate to hold cattle for feeding and sorting. Doctoring was accomplished with a heavy metal adjustable chute and a manual squeeze chute. The new horse corrals near the barn were the traditional cedar posts and poles.

Natalie Heller

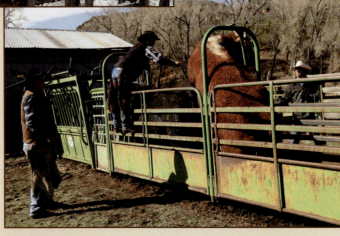

Chapter 10: Saving Centennial

The clean up was simple enough, but a monumental task. Nonetheless, we could handle it with our own small workforce. We worked for the next 11 years on that effort.

Line Cabin

Our first new construction project at Centennial was a log cabin with an adjacent outhouse. The line cabin was located just some 50 feet from the river. I stayed there during my frequent visits while still working and living in California.

This cabin gets its name and design inspiration from the rustic cabins built on large western ranches more than a century ago. These cabins were built to provide shelter and basic foodstuffs to the cowboys working near the fence "line." Often these perimeter fences would be 10 miles or more from the ranch homestead, making returning there each evening impractical.

Exterior Design

The line cabin was built in a classic western style with massive weathered standing-dead spruce logs, which were hand-notched with axe-cut ends. The handcrafted windows have traditional small panes, adding to the building's authenticity. There is a well and hand pump in the yard for water. Hand-forged wrought ironwork featuring the ranch logo with the star-in-circle motif (from the Texas Ranger badge) is attractive and functional.

Rafael Routson

Roger Wade

Chapter 10: Saving Centennial

ROGER WADE

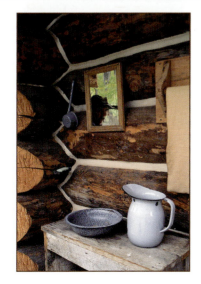

107

Interior Design

Just like the line cabins of a century ago, this one has no electricity or plumbing. Kerosene lamps and candles provide light. The stone fireplace and wood-burning cook stove provide heat.

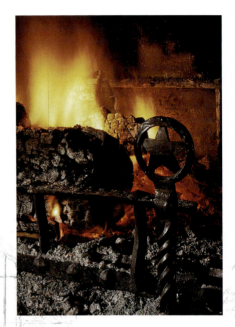

CHRIS MARONA

Great Room

The fireplace is built of native sandstone quarried near the ranch; the fireplace screen is hand-forged wrought iron as are the fireplace tools, andirons and grate.

The candle-lit chandelier depicts all the cattle brands (12) that have been used on the ranch since it was first homesteaded.

The Irish Famine chairs (circa 1850) were of reduced height common to all famine chairs, which permitted the people to sit closer to the peat fires. The chairs were so named because they were made and used during the Irish potato famine (circa 1845-1852).

Kitchen Area

The wood-burning cook stove of black cast iron and nickel (circa 1910), is the only cooking appliance in the cabin; it came from my hometown of Julesburg, Colorado.

The kitchen houses an antique butcher block (circa 1940), along with an antique American doughboy pie cabinet with curved flour and sugar bins.

The sturdy shelf above the windows, supported with aspen branch corbels, is the only storage in the cabin and is where we place things such as:

-A rare Winchester ice cream mixer (circa 1925)

-Antique boxes and tins

-A butter churn

-Bamboo fly rods and wicker creels

Dining Area

A rustic English "sawbuck" type trestle table (circa 1850) provides a place to eat off metal plates and drink from tin cups. A matching pair of English country benches with back rests and open arms are on either side of the table. The benches are pine, have shaped rear styles, exposed mortise-and-tenon construction, and plank seats (circa 1860).

The Irish dresser has three shelves over an attached base with two drawers and two doors on the bracket feet. This piece is made of wormy pine (circa 1860). The china is "Blue Willow."

Bunk Room

Through a heavy door from the great room is a cozy, low-ceiling bunk room that accommodates two single beds, a pine Dutch wardrobe, pine bedside chests, a corner antique washstand and a Victorian women's toiletry set on the shelf above the window.

Loft

Above the bunkroom is an attic loft to accommodate overflow kids and guests.

Of Special Note, Francis Whitaker, a legendary blacksmith, was a friend of mine and frequently stayed in the line cabin and at the Last Dollar Ranch where he completed a commission of a chandelier and several sconces. Francis passed away in 1999 at the age of 92.

Whitaker's obituary was printed in the November 5, 1999, edition of the *Los Angeles Times*. It read in part, "He was a hero to blacksmiths across the country for a lifetime devoted to preserving an almost lost craft and raising the standards of the blacksmith's art."

The federal government came as close as it could to declaring him a national cultural treasure in 1997. The National Endowment for the Arts honored Whitaker at the White House as one of 11 National Heritage Fellows, one of the few remaining NEA prizes earmarked for individuals.

Original Cabin, Now a Calving Shed

This cabin, built circa 1880, was originally located about 100 feet west of where Dashwood House sits today. It was in the river's flood plain before the Ridgway Reservoir was completed, so the cabin was moved to its current location on higher ground in the 1930s.

It was constructed with round logs that were later hewn flat and then covered with board-and-batten lumber on the outside, as so many frontier cabins were. The reason behind the effort required to clad the logs was two-fold; first, this treatment provided better insulation; and second, it disguised the fact it was a log building. At the time, log houses were the ultimate in "low-cost housing" and, therefore, a sensitive issue to many pioneer women. Likewise, the interior of the logs was hewn flat and lath-and-plaster applied for a smooth finish.

The original Smiths at the ranch raised nine children in this cabin, so we made every effort to preserve it. It now houses facilities, supplies and medicine for the adjacent shed where we "doctor" cows and their newborn calves.

Entrance Gate

As the highway bisects Centennial, and as we were indeed a small ranch, we needed a commanding entrance gate to make the ranch appear substantial.

Chapter 10: Saving Centennial

Barn

Ours is a classic western-style barn with long sloping shed roofs, timber-frame construction, a board-and-batten exterior, clerestory windows above the central aisle and a cedar shake roof.

It is a working ranch barn scaled for heavy draft horses—providing stalls, hay lofts, a tack and harness room, a grain room, a loafing bay for horses and a shed bay for horse-drawn wagons and implements.

The Douglas fir timber for this barn was recycled from posts and beams salvaged from the Royal Typewriter Company's manufacturing building in Hartford, Connecticut. Constructed in 1907, the facility was closed in 1972.

The Ouray National Historic District declared the barn a "historical barn" in 1995, the year it was built.

113

Volume 4: The Golden Years

Center Aisle

The center aisle is open to the roof. On each side of the main aisle, above the horse stalls and tack and grain rooms, is a loft for storing hay. The center aisle provides access from the horse corrals to the barn for:

- Cross-tying

- Harnessing

- Harness storage

- Shoeing

Draft horse stalls flank the center aisle.

Natalie Heller

Natalie Heller

Tack and Harness Room

This is the heart of the barn. Principal objects are saddle stands cantilevered from the wall supporting western roping saddles (with ropes, saddle bags and slickers) and hooks for bridles and paraphernalia necessary to operate a horse-oriented working cattle ranch. This room is home to an antique parlor log stove (Comstock Castle & Co., design patented 1875), which keeps the place inviting during winter mornings.

Roger Wade

Rafael Routson

Rafael Routson

Volume 4: The Golden Years

Winter Feeding

Winter feeding was accomplished with a team of draft horses. Before sun-up on cold winter mornings, we would light the tack room stove, harness the horses, hitch the team to the hay rack, which was loaded with nearly two tons of hay, and head out to feed the cows and their calves. When morning chores were completed, we would return to the barn and neighboring ranchers would gather in this warm tack room to drink "cowboy coffee" from tin cups and solve the world's problems. The coffee pot sits on the stove to be replenished with more grounds and water as needed.

Loafing Shed

Located on the west side of the barn, this bay allows the horses to get out of the weather and to eat hay from the manger. The hay can be dropped directly from the loft above.

Wagon Bay

Located on the east side of the barn, this covered shed is used to park and shelter horse-drawn equipment. It also includes a loading dock for barn supplies.

Chapter 10: Saving Centennial

Antique Signs, Colorado License Plates, Cast Iron Seats and Winchester Hatchets

The barn walls provide a home for my collection of antique signs, cast iron seats from early horse-drawn implements, and a variety of antique tools from yesteryear. There is also a display of numerous Colorado license plates—up to the year 1960. I collected each piece of memorabilia, personally.

117

CHRIS MARONA

Dashwood House

This was our (myself and Joan's) permanent residence. We moved in during the spring of 2003.

Dashwood House was named as a tribute to Joan's maternal history. An Aussie, Joan proudly had "Dashwood" as her middle name. Dashwood is a distinguished family name that traces its history back to medieval England. Historians note that in 1066, at the Battle of Hastings when the Normans invaded the Saxons, the Dashwood family was engaged in the conflict. The historic Dashwood crest is emblazoned on the stained glass window in the inglenook adjacent to the fireplace in the great room.

Dashwood House Grounds

A pole fence defines the grounds and keeps the livestock out. Large moss-covered boulders collected from the ranch are interspersed with native Colorado blue spruce, aspen, cottonwoods and plantings that include potentilla, sage, penstemon, columbine, wild geraniums and wild roses. A small stream from irrigation runoff runs under the house and through the garden.

The entry gate to Dashwood House is used as an introduction to the building. Stone, brick, wrought iron, art glass and timber-frame elements are fitted to the site of cliffs, river and meadows.

Design

Sited in a meadow on a long bend in the river, the building is oriented to take maximum advantage of the majestic San Juan Mountain view to the south and the Uncompahgre River and sheer canyon walls to the east.

The home was built in the American Craftsman style with western ranch/lodge and medieval English influences. It is a "timber-frame" or "post-and-beam" structure that capitalizes on the use of massive timbers salvaged from the Long Bell Sawmill in southwest Washington. The Douglas fir trees were harvested in the 1920s from the adjacent virgin forest where the trees grew to 12' in diameter and more than 200' in height.

The use of natural colors throughout the exterior, the exposed timber frame, the roof, and the stone integrate with the mature cottonwoods, the meadow and the towering cliffs in the background.

Timber Frame

All the timber in Dashwood House is recycled. It was fashioned into a timber frame by Bensonwood Homes of New Hampshire, incorporating mortise-and-tenon connections with multi-keyed cherry wood splices, oak pegged joinery, and stacked timbers with cherry wood shear keys to create a solid frame with massive timbers and multiple knee braces.

The Long Bell Sawmill during construction

Hardware

Perhaps the most unique feature of Dashwood House (along with the line cabin and barn) is the incorporation of beautiful, functional, hand-forged wrought iron hardware designed by Ted Moews and crafted by superb blacksmiths under the guidance of Howard McCall. In Dashwood House, this hardware consists of a medieval theme featured on doors, fireplaces, sconces, chandeliers and in various places in the kitchen and throughout the house.

Flooring

The southern yellow pine flooring and wainscot was recovered from the Monadnock Mill, a woolen mill complex along the Sugar River in New Hampshire. Originally constructed in the 1840s, the building from which the material was salvaged served as the complex's wheel and pump house. A dam upstream from the building diverted a flume of water to a water wheel which connected to a turbine in the bottom floor. A series of belts and shafts powered the milling machinery.

Stone

The majority of the stone used in the construction of Dashwood House was quarried adjacent to the ranch. The ammonite fossils in the great room fireplace are more than one million years old. Arkansas stone was also used in some of the masonry features to add diversity of color and texture to the stonework.

Chapter 10: Saving Centennial

Bricks

The bricks for the mud room floor and kitchen fireplace were salvaged from a century-old warehouse in Denver that was demolished to make room for the Pepsi Sports Center.

Porte-cochère

Pronounced "PORT koh SHARE," this covered main entrance to Dashwood House is a good example of the complex timber joinery, wrought-iron hardware, stone and bricks used in the house.

Front Entry

Framing the door is a flattened stone arch composed of alternating height, tapered arch stones and flanked by cut quoins.

The heavy planked doors provide an introduction to the medieval design elements used throughout the home. The custom wrought iron hinges are tapered, chamfered, hand planished, and consist of overlapping layers of strap iron pierced with cut-away areas.

The lever latches were designed specifically for this home. A simple push on the handle raises the heavy iron draw bar inside and allows one to enter the home.

Mud Room

Used brick paving, set on herringbone, provides the ideal flooring for handling wet/muddy boots and for heavy use. Along the exterior wall are heavy timber benches integrated into the timber frame where everyone can sit down and pull off their boots.

Scattered throughout the room are all the paraphernalia of a working ranch supported by wrought iron coat and hat hooks.

An antique Irish wood trough on the floor, probably from the 16th or 17th century, was originally a building timber and later hewn into a pig trough. It is a good receptacle for winter gloves.

Roger Wade

Gallery

In the first portion of this gallery are professionally produced photographs of the Double Shoe Cattle Company's two ranches—Last Dollar and Centennial.

Most of the framed pictures are from numerous Marlboro shoots at the Last Dollar. More images for Marlboro ads have been shot at the Last Dollar than at any other ranch in the United States. Images of Marlboro ads shot at Centennial are displayed elsewhere.

Roger Wade

Kitchen

As in most ranch homes, the mudroom opens to the kitchen area—the heart and soul of the home—and the center of almost all social gatherings. This kitchen combines the elements of classic English country kitchens with early American pioneer and ranch kitchens.

The kitchen flooring is slate tile from India in the color of "Indian Sunrise."

The Rumford-style brick fireplace is set at countertop height and is provisioned for open hearth cooking. Functional hand-forged wrought iron elements of the fireplace include:

- Pivoting crane with adjustable "S" hooks
- Andirons with a special attachment for coffee/pot warmer (copper pot on the warmer)
- Fire grate

Flanking the open fireplace on the right are the custom-designed fireplace tools, which include the traditional shovel, brush and poker.

Further to the right, the bread oven has hand-forged and hand-planished doors, pintle hinges and a pivoting latch.

The fireplace complex includes various niches designed for functional purposes. The niche below the raised hearth provides firewood storage; an open niche above and to the right houses an antique French mantle clock (circa late 19th century) that is flanked by two antique sitting English Staffordshire dogs (circa late 19th century).

Volume 4: The Golden Years

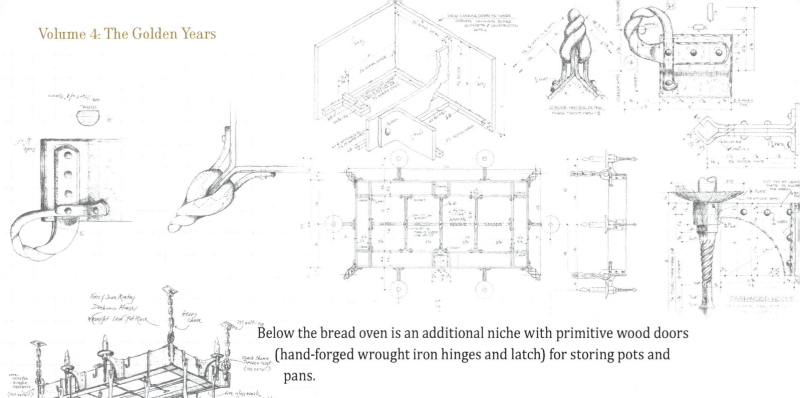

Below the bread oven is an additional niche with primitive wood doors (hand-forged wrought iron hinges and latch) for storing pots and pans.

The kitchen table is in the foreground. This is an antique English pine table with two drawers and turned legs (circa 1850). Around the table is a set of antique country chairs from rural northern England with one matching grandfather's armchair—the original finish was beech wood with ash wood seats (circa 1850).

The kitchen cabinetry is designed in Craftsman style using Douglas fir with southern yellow pine paneling. The knobs and pulls are hand forged. Cathedral glass panels were utilized in the upper cabinet doors.

An antique English butcher block on a two-drawer chest base (circa 1860) is inset into the kitchen island on the fireplace end. The top is heavily worn from use.

The pot rack above the island is custom hand-forged wrought iron with candelabra and down lights supporting antique and modern copper cookware.

The stove hood is custom wrought iron and hammered copper.

Great Room

The design consists of massive Douglas fir recycled timber for the high center poles with side aisles. Elements include:

- An elaborate timber frame with mortise-and-tenon joinery
- The four main posts are 12" x 28"
- Use of double knee braces
- Compound beams with cherry wood shear blocks
- Cherry wood splines
- King posts
- Compound diagonal bracing

Also of particular note are the hand-forged wrought iron sconces on the vertical posts. One of the primary design criteria of these sconces was to create a visual transition from the living area to the complex timber frame soaring overhead. The hand-blown glass flutes are housed in torchéres and cantilevered from the wrought-iron lattice.

The Craftsman-style fireplace has custom hand-forged wrought iron compound fireplace doors (consisting of outer glass and inner fire screen door layers). The fireplace is constructed mostly from rock quarried on or near the ranch with some ammonite fossils. A recessed area above the

mantle frames the painting "The Card Players" (circa 1971) by celebrated Australian outback artist, Hugh Sawrey, 1923-1999. The niches flanking the painting were designed to accommodate two bronze sculptures produced for us by Ted Moews (*The "Buffalo Hunter" and "Hugh Glass and the Grizzly"*).

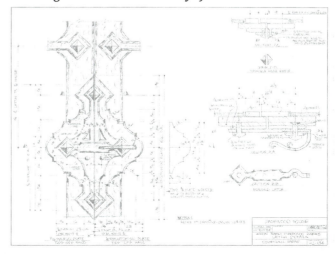

Inglenook

A reading area flanks the fireplace on the left. A custom stained-glass window depicting the Dashwood family code of arms highlights this cozy nook, while a complementary stained glass window completes the setting.

The seating in the inglenook is designed to pull out and convert into a changing table for infant grandchildren. Timber frame joinery in the seating area has cherry wood pegs and faceted heads set on the diamond.

Dining Room

The slightly more formal appearance of the dining room is enhanced with the use of a coffered ceiling and stop chamfers on the beams. A plate shelf set at clerestory height surrounds the room on two sides.

The refectory table along with the matching wooden benches was custom made for us in Australia. It is crafted of rare Kauri wood from New Zealand, which was recycled from the bulkhead of a square-rigged sailing ship.

A custom hand-forged wrought iron oval chandelier—designed by Ted Moews to complement the rectilinear nature of the dining room, table and ceiling—hangs over the table. The "bridle" above the chandelier was used to create a transition from chandelier to ceiling.

An antique pine "dog kennel" Welsh dresser displays a portion of Joan's English Staffordshire collection. Some of the pieces can also be seen mounted on the walls and on the plate shelf. The collection dates from the 19th to early 20th century. The framed pictures displayed in the dining room are English antiques.

Chapter 10: Saving Centennial

Office

Recycled timber from the Long Bell Mill in its original weathered condition gives this area a comfortable, more rustic appeal. Hand-plastered walls, a weathered barnwood ceiling, and subtle indirect lighting all enhance this massive timber frame room.

Library Loft

The heavy, recycled Douglas fir stairs provide access to the library; they are fitted with wrought iron balusters in the railing (the balusters are chamfered, planished, split, twisted, set on the chevron and hand riveted).

A custom pendant chandelier contains art-glass panels; chamfered, riveted, open work, swept finials; heavy hand-forged chain and a hand-forged "bridle."

The coffee table is an antique Irish "monk's settle." This piece was originally designed to serve three functions—bench, table and bed. It was commonly used as a seat or a bench with the top raised, then converted to a table by lowering the back, and finally used as a bed for the monk (Kilkenny, Ireland, circa 1840). The Craftsman-style fieldstone fireplace with flattened arch was constructed with quoin stones and a massive one-piece stone mantle.

Guest Bedrooms

Flanking the library are two guest bedrooms with adjoining children's play lofts. The attic-like ambiance is created by the low timber-frame gabled ceiling, which gives these rooms comfortable childhood memories. The rooms are furnished with various pieces of antique furniture and quilts from my collection—handmade by a friend of my mother's from my childhood hometown of Julesburg, Colorado.

Shortly after we moved to the ranch in 2003, it was featured in *Architectural Digest*, June 2004 issue. This article is reprinted on the following pages.

Architectural Digest | June 2014

The troubling reality of today's West is this: Ranching, as a sustainable economic enterprise, is in rapid and inexorable decline. A combination of soaring land values and labor costs, plunging beef prices and innumerable changes in what might be called lifestyle habits are eroding one of America's oldest and most august relationships between man–and animals–and the land. To put it plainly: For a ranch to survive in the modern world, it had better be owned by someone with vast reserves of mettle, unbridled passion and deep pockets.

Vince Kontny has ranching in his blood. He was born and raised in the northeast corner of Colorado, the ninth of 10 children, His father was a cattleman who foretold the future. "You can't make it ranching," he told his son.

Chapter 10: Saving Centennial

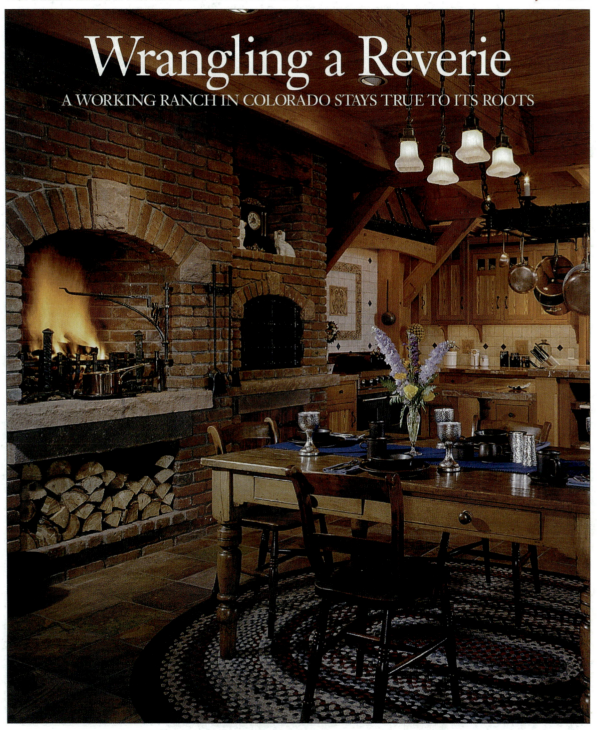

ARCHITECTURAL DIGEST
THE INTERNATIONAL MAGAZINE OF INTERIOR DESIGN
JUNE 2004

Wrangling a Reverie
A WORKING RANCH IN COLORADO STAYS TRUE TO ITS ROOTS

129

Wrangling a Reverie

A WORKING RANCH IN COLORADO STAYS TRUE TO ITS ROOTS

Architectural and Interior Design by Ted Moews/Architecture by Randall S. Walter of Bensonwood Homes/Text by Michael Frank/Photography by Roger Wade

RIGHT: The massive entrance gate to Centennial Ranch in Ridgway, Colorado, owned and operated by Vince and Joan Kontny since 1992. The couple restored some of the original buildings and erected others. "Having a ranch has been a dream of mine," says Vince Kontny.

BELOW: Dashwood House, on the banks of the Uncompahgre River, was made with recycled timbers and salvaged bricks. OPPOSITE: A post-and-beam-framed stair and custom hand-forged iron elements define the great room. Pawel Kontny, a relative, painted the hanging artworks.

The troubling reality of today's West is this: Ranching, as a sustainable economic enterprise, is in rapid and inexorable decline. A combination of soaring land values and labor costs, plunging beef prices and innumerable changes in what might be called lifestyle habits are eroding one of America's oldest and most august relationships between man—and animals—and the land. To put it plainly: For a ranch to survive in the modern world, it had better be owned by someone with vast reserves of mettle, unbridled passion and deep pockets.

Vince Kontny has ranching in his blood. He was born and raised in the northeast corner of Colorado, the ninth of 10 children. His father was a cattleman who foretold the future. "You can't make it ranching," he told his son. "Get

Chapter 10: Saving Centennial

The great room. "What we have is an eclectic mix of old beams—they became almost a found sculpture," says Ted Moews, who designed the house, with architect Randall S. Walter, as well as several outbuildings. *The Card Players*, circa 1971, is by Hugh Sawrey. Stickley armchairs; Ralph Lauren Home wing chair.

Chapter 10: Saving Centennial

yourself an education, see something of the world, then, if you still want to, come back." This is precisely what Kontny has done. Educated as an engineer, he spent the bulk of his career with the Fluor Corporation, a global engineering and construction company, from which he retired as president and COO in 1994. Never in all this time did he lose sight of, or touch with, his origins. He bought his first Colorado ranch, Last Dollar, in 1989. In 1992 he acquired the nearby Centennial Ranch. Each spread contains about 400 acres. In recent years Kontny and his wife, Joan, have spent considerable time and energy bringing these places back—not to what they were, exactly, but to what they might have been.

It's all too fitting that dozens of Marlboro ads have been shot at the Kontnys' ranches, which are in Ridgway, midway between Montrose and Telluride, in the southwest corner of the state. They are ranches in their ideal—even idealized—form. Centennial in particular has a picture-book beauty, while still functioning as a working ranch. Its land was first homesteaded in 1879. A single historic building, a log house that dates from the following year, has been restored and converted to a calv-

LEFT: A portion of Joan Kontny's 19th- and early-20th century Staffordshire collection is displayed in a Welsh dresser in the dining room. The paintings are English. BELOW: In the attic guest room is a Victorian-style four-poster. A small door leads to a children's play loft.

ing shed. Other outbuildings, imagined and executed with great fidelity to historical models, include a timber-framed draft horse barn and a spruce-log line cabin.

Centennial's centerpiece, however, is its main house, called Dashwood, after Joan Kontny's family: She is an Australian of English descent. Vince Kontny likes to describe it as "English country–cum–western ranch." It has been his dream child for many years, though it went up in just two.

BELOW: The line cabin, where the Kontnys lived during the construction of Dashwood House, has no running water or electricity. Situated in a remote area of the 400-acre property—a working ranch since 1879—the cabin is also used by ranch hands during calving season. ABOVE: Immense standing-dead spruce logs, like those in the bunk room, were used to build the structure. RIGHT: The kitchen area, with some of Vince Kontny's western and ranch memorabilia. "I've gotten a kick out of collecting these things," he says. "They're my heritage."

Having a career's experience as an executive has taught Kontny about the importance of delegation. Several men were essential to the creation of his house. Ted Moews, the first, grew up in Colorado and Wyoming. He too has ranching in his blood. But he also has a background in art, architecture, design, local history and archaeology. He draws, paints, sculpts, imagines new buildings and restores old ones. Moews listened to Vince Kontny's dreams and produced a ream of sketches in response. "He asked me to lay out a house in the best relation to the nearby Uncompahgre River, the mountains and the light. He wanted it to embrace his and Joan's personal history, too. This led me to an Arts and Crafts approach, where the fondness for the handcrafted and medieval was a link to Joan's family, and the timber-frame construction was a connection to Vince's career."

For Moews and Kontny alike, the house needed to display an honesty of materials and express pride of place. It

Chapter 10: Saving Centennial

"I wanted to restore this place to its historical significance and do what I could to protect the legacy of western ranching," notes Vince Kontny. TOP: The draft horse barn has long, sloping roofs, a timber-frame construction, clerestory windows and a board-and-batten exterior. ABOVE: Western roping saddles fill the tack and harness room. The antique parlor stove faces seating made from stumps fitted with antique cast-iron wagon seats and horseshoe footrests. RIGHT: The loading platform provides covered storage for early farm equipment.

Chapter 10: Saving Centennial

It's all too fitting that dozens of Marlboro ads have been shot at the Kontnys' ranches. They are ranches in their ideal—even idealized—form.

Moews listened to Vince Kontny's dreams. "He asked me to lay out a house in the best relation to the Uncompahgre River, the mountains and the light."

also needed to function as a building where guys could walk in with dirty boots and hang up their chaps and saddles. "I always loved the farmhouses of my youth," Vince Kontny recalls. "The way you came in through the back door to a mudroom and went from there into the kitchen." At Centennial the mudroom grew into a fairly grand but nevertheless durable place of transition. The kitchen is the undeniable heart of the house, but, following contemporary fashion, it stands in open relationship to the great room. Separate wings flank this large soaring space and contain a dining room, an office, a sitting room and bedrooms.

The house's most impressive feature is its timber-frame construction. On this Kontny and Moews collaborated with architect Randall S. Walter. He and the craftspeople at New Hampshire–based Bensonwood Homes then came to Colorado and in six days raised the house's frame; in another six they put on the roof and wall panels. The timbers were salvaged from the Long Bell

The ranch "has turned out to be a center of gravity for our family and friends," says Joan Kontny. "It really is our life now. Our life and our world." ABOVE: Near the river's edge is a hand-hewn table set among the cottonwoods, next to a cedar-post-and-lodgepole-pine fence.

Sawmill in Longview, Washington, which went up in the 1920s. "Bill Gates got the pick of the litter," Vince Kontny says. "We got the timber with character."

That it has, in spades. Some of the Douglas fir spans are 24 inches square. Others are more than 70 feet long. They have a Brobdingnagian heft relieved by handcrafted joinery that is to wood what lacework is to thread. *Mortise, tenon, peg*—these old words, and ways, rule.

The handcrafted doesn't stop here. The floors are also of salvaged wood (southern yellow pine, from an 1840s mill in New Hampshire). The wrought iron hinges, locks, pulls, sconces, chandelier and more were all designed by Moews, then engineered and hand-forged by Howard McCall, an executive who took to blacksmithing in his retirement, or other craftspeople. The remainder of the work on the house was contracted and supervised by Duane Beamer, a finish carpenter who in his spare time (what remains of it) is the ranch manager.

As for the furniture and decoration, the Kontnys were lucky; they'd traveled

> "Bill Gates got the pick of the litter. We got the timber with character."

and shopped during an adventuresome lifetime. Joan Kontny likes her Staffordshire; Vince Kontny, his old western implements, tools and memorabilia—but he has a fondness for English and Irish pieces too, "anything that respects the wood," he says, "and whose soul you can see with the eye and touch with the hand."

The interiors were organized and arrayed with newly commissioned elements (such as the great room's stained-glass windows) by the polymath Moews. "In the West we're lucky in several ways," he explains. "Ranching may be on the decline, but at least there are guys like Vince, whose land is protected by a conservation easement, which means it remains a ranch in perpetuity. And there's a great ethos in these parts among craftsmen. Vince's house expresses all this to a tee. It's a contemporary building that belongs to the 21st century but pays homage to an incredible past." □

Protection of Centennial in Perpetuity

"As long as the grass grows and the rivers flow"

Joan and I started pursuing a conservation easement for Centennial Ranch within a couple years after our purchase with the same conservation objectives we had established for Last Dollar Ranch (see Chapter 6), namely:

- Open space
- Wildlife habitat
- Agriculture production

Having received our education on the protection of Last Dollar, the effort on Centennial was easier. One difference was our selection of the land trust to hold the conservation easement.

The oldest cattleman's association in the nation is the Colorado Cattlemen's Association, founded in 1867. In 1995, this organization formed their own land trust to serve Colorado ranchers—the Colorado Cattlemen's Agricultural Land Trust (CCALT). We would be the first ranch out of the box for this land trust.

Mission: *The Colorado Cattlemen's Agricultural Land Trust protects Colorado's agriculture land, heritage and families for future generations by conserving working rural landscapes.*

On 15 November 1995, we signed the "Deed of Conservation Easement for the Centennial Ranch." With provisions for limited future owner and labor housing, the restrictions on development are similar to those established for Last Dollar. To illustrate, I will pull some quotes from the deed:

- "Use of the Property. It is the intention of the Grantors to preserve the ability of the Property to be agriculturally productive, including continuing farming and ranching activities, as well as to preserve the open space character and scenic qualities of the Property..."

- "Prohibited Acts. The Grantors promise that they will not perform, nor knowingly allow others to perform, any act on or affecting the Property that is inconsistent with the covenants below..."

- "Construction of Buildings and Other Structures. The construction of any building or other structure, except those existing on the date of this Deed or those approved by the Grantee subsequent to the date hereof but prior to construction, is prohibited..."

    - "Fences. Existing fences may be repaired and replaced, and new fences may be built anywhere on the Property for purposes of reasonable and customary management of livestock and wildlife..."

    - "Agricultural Structures and Improvements. New buildings and improvements to be used solely for agricultural purposes including the processing or sale of farm products predominantly grown or raised on the Property may be built within the building envelopes..."

    - "Single-Family Residential Dwellings. All existing single-family residential dwellings may be repaired, reasonably enlarged (not to exceed 25% of their current size) and replaced without further permission of the Grantee. Two new single-family residential dwellings, together with reasonable appurtenances such as garages and sheds, may be built on the Property below the bluff which separates the Uncompahgre River from Highway 550 within the residential building envelope..."

    - "Farm Labor and Tenant Housing. All existing dwellings or structures used to house farm tenants and employees may be repaired, reasonably enlarged (not to exceed 25% of their current size), and replaced at their current location without further permission of the Grantee. Three new single or multi-family dwellings or structures to be used solely to house farm tenants, employees, or others engaged in agricultural production on the Property ("Employee Housing Buildings") may be built on the Property..."

    - "Ranch Office Building. A new building, which may not be used for residential purposes, which is intended to be used as a ranch office building, and which shall not exceed 1,500 square feet of gross floor area, may be constructed within the agricultural building envelope..."

-"Repair and Replacement. All buildings which are permitted to be constructed hereunder may be repaired, reasonably enlarged (not to exceed 25% of their permitted size), and replaced at their permitted location..."

- "Subdivision. Title to the Property shall not be divided or subdivided, it being the intent of the Grantors herein that the Property shall remain intact as a single parcel..."

- "Trash. The dumping or accumulation of any kind of trash or refuse on the Property, other than farm-related trash and refuse produced on the Property, is strictly prohibited..."

- "Recreational Uses. Golf courses, airstrips, and helicopter pads are strictly prohibited on the Property..."

- "Feed Lot. The establishment of a commercial feed lot is prohibited..."

- "Water Rights. The Grantors shall retain and reserve the right to use water rights sufficient for use in agricultural production on the Property, and shall not transfer, encumber, lease, sell, or otherwise separate such quantity of water rights from title to the Property itself..."

- "Rights Retained by the Grantors. Subject to interpretation under paragraph 21, as owners of the Property, the Grantors retain the right to perform any act not specifically prohibited or limited by this Deed. These ownership rights include, but are not limited to, the right to exclude any member of the public from trespassing on the Property and the right to sell or otherwise transfer the Property to anyone they choose..."

For future generations, this conservation easement will ensure this small piece of the West will remain as it is today — forever.

Chris Marona

A Day in the Life of Centennial, Circa 1935

Introduction

As was portrayed in *Chapter 7: A Day in the Life of Last Dollar*, illustrating a typical day's activities at the ranch during a winter and summer day in 1935, with Duane Beamer and Ted Moews, I have attempted to do likewise for Centennial Ranch. My apologies in advance for any inaccuracies due to poor research.

1935 was yet another difficult year in America; the end of the Great Depression was not in sight. Those in agriculture could, presumably, weather the country's hardships easier than those in urban areas since, at the time, they were quite self-sufficient for life's basic needs of food and shelter.

At Centennial Ranch, life during those trying times was less of a struggle than it was at the much higher elevated Last Dollar Ranch.

Winter

When: Wednesday, 6 February 1935

Where: The Smith Place, approximately 12 miles south of Montrose along the Uncompahgre River at an elevation of 6,439'.

The temperature at night generally was in the range of +10°F to +20°F, but with a cold spell, could easily dip to -15°F. Early this morning the thermometers on the house read 12°F. With some sunshine and a few clouds, it should get up to 45°F by noon.

In the simple white, wood-framed three-bedroom house were Ralph (the son of the pioneer, James Smith), his wife Rose, their sons (Jim, 23; Verle, 21; and Rollen, 15) and their only daughter, Louise (16).

It was about 5:30 a.m. before Ralph and Rose left their warm bed to get the fires stoked to heat the house. They beat the sun up by more than two hours. The primary heating stove in the dining, living and family rooms was the popular, efficient, mid-priced Round Oak Potbelly stove, Model K-16. Attractive, black cast iron with ample nickel-plated features, it was first and foremost practical. It had a flat top to accommodate a large pot of water to humidify the dry air and to provide a handy source of hot water for washing up and shaving (accomplished with a badger hair soap brush and a straight razor with the leather strap handy for frequently sharpening).

For the Collins family, fuel for the stove was supplied with a soft, friable coal mined from a horizontal adit[1] dug into a steep mountain just about three miles up Billy Creek, which entered the river immediately south of the Smith Place. It was a one-man mine with the mined coal piled near the entrance for locals to buy by the wagon-load and, on slow days, to be delivered by the miner with his team and dirty wagon.

Ralph had constructed his coal bin next to the house just steps from the back door (there was a front door, which was seldom, if ever, used). The bin was big enough to accommodate a wagonload of coal. It consisted of two separate compartments—the much larger of the two would hold small lumps and all the fines[2] and the other bin was reserved for the larger pieces, weighing a few pounds apiece.

---

1 An adit (from Latin aditus, entrance) is an entrance to an underground mine which is horizontal or nearly horizontal, by which the mine can be entered, drained of water, ventilated, and minerals extracted at the lowest convenient level. Adits are also used to explore for mineral veins.

2 Coal fines: Coal with a maximum particle size usually less than one-sixteenth inch and rarely above one-eighth inch.

> Ralph, his father, James, and his three sons were cattlemen pure and simple. Beef was their singular product. So they looked like and had all the skills of real cowboys.

The sizable lumps were reserved for the potbelly stove to be added at bedtime. The coal would slowly burn through the night, keeping the house at a reasonable temperature (approx 60°F).

The wood cookstove was allowed to burn out at night with Rose lighting kindling to get it going first thing every morning. Firewood was preferred for this stove since it was much easier to control the heat on the stovetop and in the oven. Like all housewives in the area (and of the era), she was a master at regulating the heat in the oven by simply testing it with her hand through the open door. Some women preferred to check the temperature with their more sensitive elbows.

This morning, Ralph shook the grate in the potbelly stove to drop some ashes but retain the hot coals. Then he added some of the finer coal from his coal-come-ash tin bucket next to the stove.

As was common in all rural households, the routine daily chores were performed before breakfast. The Collins' kept three or four milk cows to provide whole milk and cream for the kitchen and skim milk for the hogs and the young calves. Either Jim or Verle, or sometimes both, would milk the cows, operate the small separator, then "slop the hogs," gather the eggs from the nearby coop, scatter some grain for the chickens, and then return to the house to satisfy their raging appetites with a hearty ranch breakfast served by Rose and Louise.

With three strong boys, it was not necessary for Ralph to employ a hired man. When more help was needed for a particular activity, a call would go out to the neighbors who always willingly pitched in. Of course, with such a supply of manpower, the Collins were frequently called to help others. After breakfast it was time to go to work.

Ralph, his father, James, and his three sons were cattlemen pure and simple. Beef was their singular product. So they looked like and had all the skills of real cowboys. Their work during the winter was to look after a sizable herd of cattle consisting of some 230 mother cows, 38 bred heifers, 32 replacement heifers and 19 bulls.

To feed and work their herd, they had 12 saddle horses and four draft horse teams. Today, as on every winter morning, Jim and Verle would harness a team, hook it on to the large hay sled, break the ice in the stock tanks, then head for the nearest hay stack on the west side of the road where they kept the majority of the cows. They would pull alongside the stack, Jim would climb on top with his pitchfork and Verle leveled the hay on the sled as Jim sent it down. Once the first load was ready, they looked for clean snow where, with the team walking slowly in a straight line, both young men would pitch the hay off the sides.

This haying operation would be repeated six more times before all the cattle were fed. They were expected to have the chore completed by noon if they wanted a hot dinner.

In the meantime, Ralph, with help from young Rollen, would tend to the horses and tack. This morning, they also replaced the shoes on two saddle horses. Ralph was an expert horseman with respected skills as a horse trader as well as a trainer for bought and bred stock. The Smiths preferred to do their heavy work with a team as opposed to a tractor, favored by most of their neighbors.

Ralph's sons, as well as Louise, were excellent horsemen. Each of the men were competent farriers, could make or repair their tack and harness and, while wrecks were common, they were especially good at breaking horses. They did much of the initial training work in a fairly small, crude round-pen about 5' high made of horizontal poles.

By noon, everyone was hungry, having burned off all the calories from breakfast. Rose and Louise had prepared a meal to satisfy a small army.

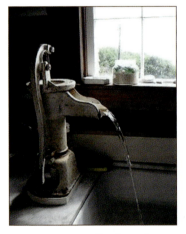

After dinner the men would take their power nap on the hardwood floor while Rose and Louise hurried through the dishes and prepared for their weekly trip into town. The Smith kitchen did not have running water, of course, but with a deep, hand dug well close to the house, they did have a kitchen sink and a hand-operated siphon pump above the sink. For the ladies, this was real luxury—along with the electric lights.

Rose prepared her list of staples she needed at the grocery. Ralph recited what he wanted from the hardware store. Both lists were brief for most foodstuffs were available on the ranch during the summer—all it needed was preservation. Likewise, the hardware list consisted only of those tools and nails that they couldn't provide. The leatherwork for halters, bridles, saddles and the harness for the draft horses they could make; only the brass buckles were required from town.

The men spent the entire afternoon breaking and training two young colts in the round pen. At that time they were undecided as to whether to keep them for the ranch or sell them. Mostly it would depend on the offer price.

They milked the cows in the late afternoon, looked after the other animals (pigs, chickens, dogs and cats), then washed up to enjoy a light supper and be in bed by 9 p.m.

Summer

When: Friday, 16 August 1935

Where - The Smith Place approximately 12 miles south of Montrose along the Uncompahgre River at an elevation of 6,493'

Today the sun came up over the cliffs along the river at 5:26 a.m. and would disappear behind the canyon wall to the west at 7:05 p.m. It would be a clear sky so blue it nearly hurt one's eyes—with just a few fluffy clouds for contrast. The temperature would be in the high 80s early in the afternoon and would dip to a pleasant low 60s by night—low enough to keep the house cool all day by simply opening the windows after supper.

Breakfast was on the table before 5 a.m.; the men needed all the daylight hours available. The cows were milked quickly, with the separating chore left for Rose and Louise. Once the hogs and three orphaned calves were fed, the day's work began.

Earlier, in June, all the cows, calves, heifers and bulls were moved some 10 to 15 miles to the west to graze on the rich grass slopes of Horsefly Peak (some 1,600 acres owned by the Smiths), and some miles further, on the Smith's Iron Springs pasture.

The Smith's heading to cow camp to repair fence.

The summer grazing elevation was over 9,000'. With some good spring rains, the cattle and the grass would have ample water. Perimeter and cross fences had to be checked and repaired before the livestock arrived, and unless an old aspen tree would fall across the fence, they should keep the cows in place. If some did manage to get through the fence before it could be fixed, the neighbors would simply hold them with their livestock until the fall gather. Therefore, it was essential that all animals in the high country be branded; any "slick" calves would be hard to claim in the fall. Besides, it was the law that all cows and calves carry their owner's mark.

The long trek with the livestock from the bottom ground to the high country was perhaps the summer's main event. It required planning not unlike a military operation. The mission was to drive more than 500 head of cows and calves some 18 uphill trail miles during a three-day trek. The calves were young so they petered out quickly if pushed too hard.

Louise and Rollen would remain below to look after the chores there. All the rest of the family would fall in. Rose, with the strongest team and biggest wagon, would trail the herd. In the wagon was ample food to restock the crude cow camp shelters and to feed the crew with a fireset and an open fire the first night—so pots and pans and a dutch oven were in the mix.

> There was another major undertaking that required the men's attention every daylight hour they could spare after their livestock and haying chores. This project was to relocate the Uncompahgre River from its present winding course through the flood plain of the ranch to its proposed new location just below the sandstone cliffs on the east side of the valley. It was a considerable undertaking with the benefit of creating more grassland and eliminating the problem of having cows with their young calves attempting to cross the river.

Bedrolls were also in the wagon, for they would be sleeping under the stars the first night. Actually, they all hoped they could see the stars during a cloudless night, which would mean "no rain." Everything needed for the trip and throughout the summer was also carefully piled into the wagon. Such items as a small anvil and a stock of shoes for the horses in case they would throw a shoe on the trip or at the cow camp later. Also included were salt blocks for the cows.

They reached the Horsefly cow camp early on the second afternoon. A spring next to the camp had been developed with a 3" pipe embedded in the slope. Clear water ran out of that pipe every day, all day, keeping a small pond full before trickling down to a lower creek.

It was a hectic afternoon sorting the livestock and doctoring any animals needing attention after the long drive. The cow camp shelter was emptied of the mice and chipmunks, cleaned and restocked with ample supplies to satisfy the needs of the cowboy who would be checking the livestock every two weeks during the summer. They would leave the heifers at the ranch along with a few bulls to keep them happy.

In the morning, the wagon and cowboys would push the cows and young calves another five miles to the Iron Springs cow camp. Once the work there was completed, and after a night's rest, they would all return to the ranch below to the seemingly never-ending task of irrigating and putting up hay.

Today, Friday, 16 August, Jim, with his saddle horse and two spares working as pack horses with panniers full of supplies, would set out before daybreak on the trip to the two cow camps to check the livestock, doctor those needing doctoring, and fixing any fence that needed fixing. He would return after 4 or 5 days when his work was completed.

The haying operation would continue today, as it would almost every day during the summer, for the amount of hay in the stacks dictated how many cows they could feed through the winter. The Smith's John Deere #8 sickle mower, two John Deere dump rakes, the buck rake, and overshot stacker were all kept busy.

There was another major undertaking that required the men's attention every daylight hour they could spare after their livestock and haying chores. This project was to relocate the Uncompahgre River from its present winding course through the flood plain of the ranch to its proposed new location just below the sandstone cliffs on the east side of the valley. It was a considerable undertaking with the benefit of creating more grassland and eliminating the problem of having cows with their young calves attempting to cross the river.

Rerouting the river was no knee-jerk plan, for it would be expensive and require a great deal of work. Last summer (1934) they started to execute their well thought-out project. The initial task was to take an axe to each of the cottonwoods in the river's new path and remove a ring of bark. This, of course, killed the tree, which was then felled last winter, piled, and burned.

Earlier this summer, in May, the real work began. For this next task, the Smiths had purchased a very used Caterpillar D4 tractor fitted with a fixed dozer blade. With the national depression still blazing, it was a considerable investment.

The boys soon mastered the basic tractor/bulldozer operating skills. Three months ago, starting at the northern (downstream) boundary of the ranch where the river returned to just below the cliff, they dozed a single ditch down the centerline of their proposed new stream bed. Then once that first pass was complete (for some 200'), they turned their dozer 90° and pushed the river gravel (consisting of river-rounded rocks of varying sizes less than about 10 pounds in weight) off to both sides to form the new river bank. It was slow, tedious work, but they were determined, putting in several hours on the dozer each day.

Finally, in early July, the new rough stream bed was complete. With great anticipation and a jubilant crowd of family and friends, Jim, with his dozer, removed the last gravel barricade. The water started with a small flow into its new stream bed. A few more passes with the dozer and the river's full capacity changed course where it would remain for the future. There was, justifiably, a great celebration with previously hidden bottles of whiskey being passed around for a long pull.

The work of containing the river in its new bed would continue for months. To keep the west bank from eroding, a call went out for junked car frames which were placed along the side of the stream.

For Rose and Louise, today was another long day of gardening, and in the afternoon, another session of canning. At this altitude, the long, warm summer days were ideal for growing the full spectrum of vegetables. Their large garden was replenished with year-old manure every spring. The fertile ground produced a virtual bounty of food.

Another benefit of the Smith Place was the fact that the climate was also suitable for growing fruit trees—apricot, cherry, chokecherries, wild plum, a variety of apples, even a few peaches. The apricot trees would bloom first in the spring, and if they survived a late freeze, would produce an abundance of small, but delicious, apricots.

Some were served at the meals, others made into thick jam and many more canned. The most popular treatment was to split the fruit, remove the seed, then set them skin side down on a large wooden flat to dry in the sun. Likewise, early and late varieties of apples received some of the same treatment with apple slices drying in the sun to be enjoyed during the long winter months. Some apples were consumed at the time of course, but others would turn into applesauce and the popular apple butter.

This day, in 1935, despite the nation's economic troubles, life was good on the Smith Place.

Chapter 13: Ranch Life

Ranch Life

It is in this chapter, with its intentional all-encompassing title, that I will attempt to provide the reader with a background on what it is like to experience life on a working cattle ranch in Southwest Colorado.

This can best be accomplished, in my opinion, through images rather than with lengthy text. So what follows is a primer of a cow-calf operation as practiced on our two ranches, and then what life was like on these ranches.

The Beef Business

In the beef cattle industry, a cow-calf outfit such as ours is known as a "producer." This is a very large, fragmented group of some 800,000 ranchers in the United States with an average herd size of just 40 head of cattle. These ranchers breed the cows and "produce" the calves.

The next segment of the industry, known as "feeders," operate feedlots where a 700-800 pound calf is fed an enriched diet of grain and hay to take the animal up to a sale weight of some 1,200 pounds in a few months. Feeders put the "finishing touches" on the animals. These feedlot operations are mostly huge in order to take full advantage of scale of production.

Natalie Heller

The last leg of this three-legged stool is the "packers" who buy the finished animal from the feedlot, then process the meat through several stages where it will eventually end up in the meat counter of your local supermarket. This segment of the industry is dominated by a handful of large, multi-national corporations.

Prices, whether for calves, finished animals out of the feedlot, or what is marked on the plastic-wrapped package of steak at the store, vary mostly as a result of supply and demand. This, of course, is influenced by the economy, international trade and environmental factors.

Brands

In Colorado, livestock owners are not required to fence their livestock in. Instead, if landowners want to keep livestock off their property, they must fence the animals out. This is commonly referred to as the "Open Range Law." Therefore, it is of interest, and is required, that all livestock owners must place a brand on the hide of animals—be they horses, cattle, mules or donkeys — their registered brand (a permanent mark registered with the state as a livestock brand).

A properly applied registered brand is proof of ownership. It is, in essence, an animal's return address should it become separated from its herd. According to past and present law, before an individual can sell his animal (horses or cows) he must contact a state-employed brand inspector to certify a legal brand is on the animal. Likewise, an unbranded animal commonly referred to as a "maverick" or "slick" can legally be sold for cash.

Within Colorado, all aspects of managing the brand requirements in the purchase, transport and sale of livestock is the responsibility of the State Board of Stock Inspection Commissioners— commonly referred to as the "Brand Board."

The Colorado Brand Board has a long proud history:

- Formed in 1865, when Colorado was still a territory
- Became a state agency in 1903
- Became a division of the Colorado Department of Agriculture in the early 1970s
- Is comprised of five members who are appointed by the governor

The Brand Board administers some 35,000 Colorado brands and periodically publishes a hardcover Colorado Brand Book identifying 30,000+ registered brands.

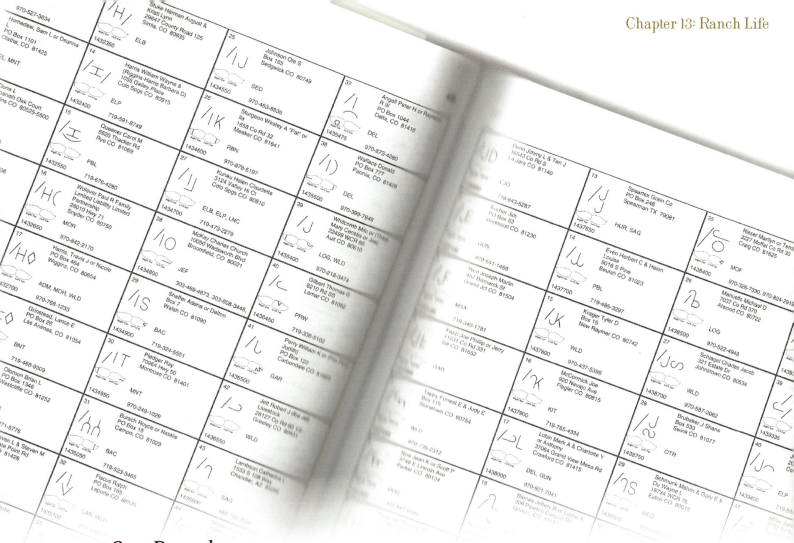

Our Brand

After we purchased Last Dollar Ranch in 1989 with the intent of raising cattle, we required a brand. There were two options: we could purchase a registered brand for sale through the Brand Board or we could work through the Brand Board to create a brand of our design which did not conflict with any of their existing brands. We did both.

For our horses, we purchased from the owner the "70" brand; inspired, according to the owners, because their ranch was 70 miles from town. My father, Ed Kontny, had a brand which I inherited since no on else in the family intended to own livestock. The brand "E backward K" simply was not a practical brand for us because there were many crossed lines, which would retain an excessive amount of heat in the iron resulting in a blotched brand on the hide. A distinctive practical brand was important to me, personally, for I wanted to incorporate the brand in the name of our envisioned cattle company.

There was, however, a big problem. Most brands satisfying our requirements had been long ago registered with the Brand Board and the owners would not even consider parting with them; even though for generations the brand most likely had never been applied to an animal hide but rather to just a T-bone steak on the grill, or occasionally, a family T-shirt.

> There are ways to get around such obstacles if one is determined and creative. In our case, we had a secret weapon in the form of Duane Beamer and his winning personality.

Ideally, I wanted a brand without any crossed lines and incorporating one, or two, upright horseshoes (upright so the "luck doesn't run out"). A tall order, since the Brand Board had publicly stated they would not issue any new "picture" brands (i.e. house, diamond, pitchfork, cross, et al).

There are ways to get around such obstacles if one is determined and creative. In our case, we had a secret weapon in the form of Duane Beamer and his winning personality. Duane's father was a long-time brand inspector, so that connection gave him a unique insight in how the Brand Board operated.

Chapter 13: Ranch Life

PHOTOS BY NATALIE HELLER

Basically, the decision-making power of the Brand Board is entrusted to the five appointed members who normally serve for a few years. So, not surprisingly, the real clout belongs to the women who have administered the Board's activities for decades. Win the hearts and minds of those ladies and great things could be accomplished.

Armed with his personality and a two-pound box of See's candies, Duane pursued his mission of obtaining a desirable brand from the Brand Board. Within two weeks we received notice of our new, registered brand. Our brand, consisting of a bar and two upright horseshoes can be read as "Bar Double Shoe," which we prefer, or "Bar Two Shoes."

Our Cattle Company

Many famous western ranches are named after the brands the animals carry (i.e. the Four Sixes Ranch in Texas). So, with our brand, we could create and name our cattle company, consisting of two ranches and all of the cattle, with a name derived from our brand. It would be forever known as the Double Shoe Cattle Company.

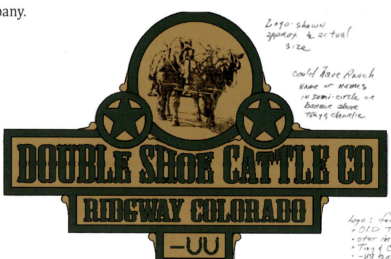

Chapter 13: Ranch Life

The Ranch Families

Several families have lived on our ranches during our tenure.

Beamer Family

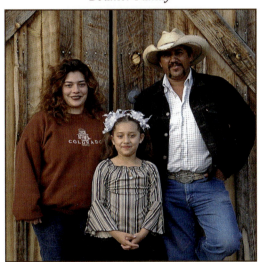
Fernandez Family

Middleton Family

Kontny Family

Weddings

Both of our daughters were married on our ranches: Natascha at Last Dollar and Amber at Centennial.

Natascha and Jan Gundersen at Last Dollar Ranch, July 5, 2003

USA Today, in its November 16, 1994, issue, published an article titled "Historic Ranch to Stay Pretty as a Picture" announcing the American Farmland Trust conservation easement. They called it, "One of the nation's most picturesque ranches seen by millions as a backdrop in magazine ads," and indeed it is.

Natascha and Jan were married on a meadow overlooking the lake and ranch homestead with the background being the San Juan Mountains. After the wedding, a reception was held at the homestead with a tent providing protection for the dinner and the adjacent log-and-stone barn serving as the dance hall.

Chapter 13: Ranch Life

Amber and Adam Cornell at Centennial Ranch, August 30, 2008

Centennial Ranch, with the beautiful Uncompahgre River running through it, was the location for our daughter Amber's wedding to Adam Cornell.

On the evening before the wedding, guests were given a taste of "Old West" hospitality with a barbecue in the timber-frame barn. Wedding guests were given a key chain featuring the circle star logo of Centennial Ranch as a favour.

The ceremony was conducted on the riverbank next to the line cabin. Following the wedding, a reception was held in a large tent adjacent to Dashwood House.

Chapter 13: Ranch Life

Cowboys

The men who have worked on our ranches for the past quarter century, where we perform all cattle work with horses where practical, are truly outstanding cowboys. They are masters of their chosen craft.

- Excellent horsemen whether working with saddle horses or our team of Belgians. We don't ride in circles on these ranches.

- They shoe their own and all the ranch horses.

- They have made, for themselves and the ranch, most of the gear required by cowboys (chaps, chinks, spurs, bits, halters or repairs necessary for saddles, bridles or harness).

- Competent in the operation and maintenance of all the equipment required on a modern working cattle ranch.

- They also possess that rare work ethic from our western heritage.

- Lastly, they have all retained a great sense of humor.

The following images will introduce you to them. They are the real deal. In fairness, some of the images that follow are of my family, not yet quite the "real deal."

Chapter 13: Ranch Life

Chris Marona

Chris Marona

Volume 4: The Golden Years

Photos by Natalie Heller

Chapter 13: Ranch Life

Photos by Natalie Heller

165

Volume 4: The Golden Years

Chris Marona

Chris Marona

Natalie Heller

Chapter 13: Ranch Life

Natalie Heller

Natalie Heller

167

Cowboy Gear

As the population of people who are familiar with cowboy gear diminishes, I thought it important to include a bit of information on the equipment cowboys use in their daily work and while on horseback in the wide open spaces. Let's start with the individual from the top down.

Hats

Cowboy hats vary somewhat by geography. In Nevada's Great Basin, for example, the preference is for a flat brim. Yet farther afield in the Australian outback, it is the Akubra in various styles. They say, "Akubra is Australian for hat." Everyone in the Outback keeps the sun off their faces with an Akubra, the vast majority of the hats without their original shape and without any hope of carrying water for their dog, but all with loads of character. My son-in-law, Jan, wears an Akubra.

Here in southwest Colorado, and all places as far south as Texas, the hat worn by the Marlboro Man is the one of choice—with a 4" brim turned up to suit the individual. A good fit is important so it stays in place during a hard run or when there is high wind. Color is a dealer's choice, but not unlike Ford who gave us the Model T, most cowboys will choose any color as long as it is black. Some will have a Sunday hat in the light-colored "Silver Belly" shade.

Always best to invest in a quality hat and amortize it over many years. Tourists like to buy a "distressed" new hat since they don't sweat.

As for the hatband, I prefer leather; almost exclusively worn by cowboys during the "Open Range" years of the 1800s. Check this out next time you watch *Lonesome Dove*.

Cowboys are also a superstitious breed. For example, they never put a hat on a bed to avoid bad luck.

NATALIE HELLER

Wild Rags

One of the cowboys' fading wardrobe items, more frequently seen at social functions than when working cattle, is the "wild rag" worn around the neck. It was a common part of a cowboys' outfit during the Open Range era where it was used for every purpose imaginable, but a great aid to shield the face from dust when riding drag or during a blizzard. It was also useful during stagecoach hold-ups, which are rare now.

Ads selling wild rags are pushing the highest quality silk in every imaginable color and print, including "charmeuse paisley tied with the bank robbers' knot."

Shirts

Again, personal preference, with patterns more popular now than the more traditional solids favored by the Marlboro Man. However, a cowboy will never wear a shirt with 13 snaps (bad luck).

Jeans

Standard cowboy issue of course, with Levi 501s and Wranglers cornering the market. Jeans are worn 1-2" long so they are "stacked" above the heel of the boot. "Cowboy designer jeans" is an oxymoron.

Vests

Should be a solid color whose sole purpose is to retain body heat. Carhartt is the brand of choice these days.

Jackets

Anything that works to insure freedom of movement and that will keep water and cold out. Filson's "Tin Cloth" or its oil skin "Cruiser" are perfect.

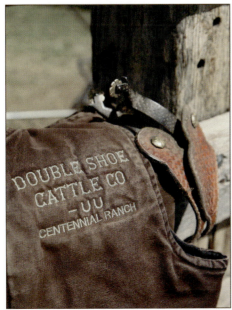

Natalie Heller

Natalie Heller

Chaps and Chinks

These are two types of a protective, leather garment used by mounted riders for protection against brush. The word "chaps" comes from the spanish word "chaparreras." They have evolved over the decades with the earliest designs being "batwings" or, in the northern area "woolies" with the fleece on the outside. Currently, the type favored by the Marlboro cowboys are the "shotgun" chaps, sometimes called "stovepipes" because the legs are straight and narrow. These are also best when riding in rainy weather or the cold. The protective leggings preferred by most cowboys on our ranches are "chinks", 3/4-length chaps that stop some 5-10" below the knee with very long fringe at the bottom and on the sides. My families chaps and chinks were made by Duane Beamer, a great leather craftsman.

Natalie Heller

Natalie Heller

Britni Branson/Krystal Russell

Chapter 13: Ranch Life

Slickers

These specialized raincoats are essential items that are tied to the back of the saddle regardless of the weather forecast. Their function—warm and dry!

Very popular are slickers from "The Australian Outback Collection" (see the movie, *The Man From Snowy River*). As for slickers preferred by the Marlboro Man, he can have any color as long as it's yellow.

Belt Buckles

Buckles should be big. We're not talking about the trophy buckles the rodeo boys wear, but rather what suits working cowboys, belly latches—often with the rancher's brand and the wearer's name engraved.

We created two excellent silver-brass buckles, one for each ranch, which we gave to people who actually contributed to the restoration and/or working of the ranches.

PHOTOS BY NATALIE HELLER

Boots

Besides the hat (to protect the head at one end), boots (to keep the feet as comfortable as possible on the other end) are the other most important piece of a cowboy's daily attire. These have a high heel, primarily to keep one's foot from going through the stirrup, which can have disastrous results. They also help a short cowboy look taller for the ladies.

The boot's height can be regular (about 12") or high (about 17"). I prefer the high boot with a "spur ridge" or "spur shelf" above the heel to keep the spur from slipping down.

My preferred boot for work, horseback or on foot, is the lace-up 10" "Packer" made by White's Boots of Spokane, Washington, again with a spur shelf. These are good in the stirrup, and with the ankle support, one can walk for miles, if need be, in comfort.

Spurs

The wearing of metal spurs on a rider's boot to help direct a horse's movements has a history that goes back centuries. The Western cowboy spur consists of a metal heal band, a shank, a rowel and a leather strap to hold it all in place. There are hundreds of versions. At our ranches, some of the cowboys make their own spurs from either round stock or a farrier's rasp.

I have a modest collection of Crockett spurs. Oscar Crockett was one of the world's "Big 3" most famous spur makers. Born in 1887, he formed the Crockett Bit and Spur Company in 1920. He moved his business to Boulder, Colorado, in 1943 where he employed up to 125 craftsmen, which makes him, in my mind, "Colorado's spur maker."

Chapter 13: Ranch Life

For many years, I wore a pair of Crockett spurs, until our foreman, Rick Hardesty, made me spurs from a broken front axle from our own 1950 Jeep.

Natalie Heller

Natalie Heller

That completes the cowboy's attire. So let's look at how he outfits his horse. The gear used on horses is collectively known as "tack."

173

Horse Gear

Saddle

All our ranch saddles, and all those owned by our hands, are sturdy roping saddles. My personal saddle is typical. I bought it decades ago from the maker, Buz Johnson of Norco, California, where he was running a large saddle shop. Buz was a dedicated team roper who, with his fellow ropers (according to him) met every Sunday afternoon to practice their sport and enjoy the camaraderie. This was his personal saddle that he had used for years—it is sturdy, heavy, with excellent leather tooling and rawhide.

Natalie Heller

Natalie Heller

Bridle

This piece of tack functions as a steering wheel and brake pedal do in a vehicle. Again, there are numerous bit designs depending on the rider's purpose and the age and temperament of the horse.

The bit I use was created from stock steel by Rafael Routson, who wrote our two award-winning ranch books (*A Ranching Legacy* and *A Heritage in Iron*). It is a magnificent bit forged with stock steel under the guidance of a master blacksmith when Rafael was in her early 20s.

Rope

The rope (aka lasso/lariat/riata) is a cowboy's best friend if he is riding in open country and must doctor a cow or calf. Its use is a hard-to-acquire skill that separates our cowboys from us wannabes. All people are familiar with its use from watching the rodeo events calf roping and team roping where mounted cowboys ensnare full-size animals.

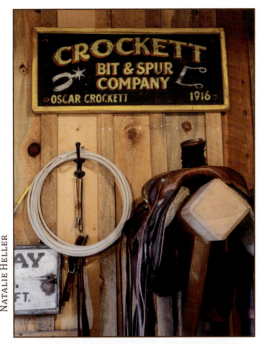

Modern lariats are made of stiff nylon or polyester and, for working cowboys, vary in length from 28-35 feet. It has a small loop at one end (hondo) through which the rope passes to form a loop that hopefully passes over a calf's head or around a cow's back legs.

Saddlebags

These are two identical, connected bags that are tied to the back of the saddle to carry such things as fencing pliers, syringes and vaccine (when checking cattle in open country), etc. Bags are essential if there is a need to carry anything.

Oddly, at least to me, our cowboys never use their saddlebags to carry water or food, even during long drives. Evidently they can wait for dinner, and as for liquid refreshments, they prefer to hydrate at the end of the day with Coors Light.

Oddly, at least to me, our cowboys never use their saddlebags to carry water or food, even during long drives. Evidently they can wait for dinner, and as for liquid refreshments, they prefer to hydrate at the end of the day with Coors Light.

Volume 4: The Golden Years

Gear from yesteryear

Natalie Heller

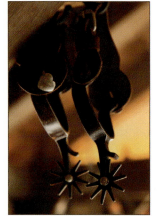

Britni Branson/Krystal Russell

Britni Branson/Krystal Russell

Chapter 13: Ranch Life

Ranch Animals

Horses

In an effort to keep our western heritage alive and because we simply prefer working with horses rather than ATVs for our cattle operation, we share with the reader some of our favorite horse images.

PHOTOS THIS PAGE BY CHRIS MARONA

177

Chris Marona

Chris Marona

Natalie Heller

Chris Marona

Chapter 13: Ranch Life

Natalie Heller

Natalie Heller

> Sic a well-trained dog onto a cantankerous cow during a cattle drive—a cow who would rather go walkabout in the bush than stay with the herd on the trail—and one has to chuckle at the resulting commotion. The cow, humbled, always returns to the herd.

Dogs

The cowboys on our ranches, and in the general area here, all seem to be of one mind when it comes to a cattle dog. First, they need them, and second, they must be a Blue Heeler. This breed, mid-sized, short-haired, energetic, intelligent, trainable and loyal to a single master, traces its history back to Australia.

In the mid 1880s, a drover who had used his dogs on the long treks of big cattle herds to market experimented with crossing them with dingoes—the wild dogs of Australia. The result, a Blue Heeler, was introduced to the United States after World War II when soldiers returning home brought them back as pets.

Natalie Heller

As their name implies, the dogs gain the respect of cows by nipping at their heels. Sic a well-trained dog onto a cantankerous cow during a cattle drive—a cow who would rather go walkabout in the bush than stay with the herd on the trail—and one has to chuckle at the resulting commotion. The cow, humbled, always returns to the herd.

Chapter 13: Ranch Life

Natalie Heller

Jason is always accompanied by his dogs (currently two and a spare) whether on foot, in a pickup, on a tractor, or on horseback. When on horseback, if one of his dogs wanders ahead of him or alongside, he will simply say "behind" to get it in the proper position, just south of his horse.

Natalie Heller

There is one more dog of a herding breed that was very much a part of our family here in Colorado. He is "Dutch." Joan, an Aussie, was a subject of her admired Queen Elizabeth. The queen has Corgies, so we had a Corgi. Excellent choice!

181

Wildlife

One of the considerations for protecting our ranches from any future development was to provide sustainable habitat for the abundant and diverse wildlife that call the ranches "home."

For our book, "A Ranching Legacy," Edward Aldrich, an internationally acclaimed wildlife artist, provided a series of pencil sketches and some paintings of animals found on Last Dollar and Centennial ranches. Some are included here along with some of our hunting and fishing shots.

Colorado's 41st Governor (from 2007 to 2011) Bill Ritter

Chapter 13: Ranch Life

Ted Moews

Ted Moews

Edward Aldrich

Edward Aldrich

Volume 4: The Golden Years

Cattle

The beef cattle business, which my family and I elected to enter after I retired from my decades-long career in international engineering and construction, was motivated more for the lifestyle than any prospect for financial return. Many small operators remain in the business because it provides independence and a satisfying and desirable existence for self and family. As for us, I say we are a "not-for-profit ranch," unintentionally!

These small outfits, say with a double-digit number of mother cows, can still make a reasonable livelihood, but only if they have inherited their land debt free and are willing to sacrifice vacations, the prospect of sending their children to out-of-state colleges, drive a 10-year-old pickup and forego the security of adequate health insurance for their family and any hired help.

The current elevated live calf prices still will not offset the rapidly escalating costs of equipment, fertilizer and other essentials. If they can beat those odds, they must still deal with crippling estate taxes when they die and want to pass the assets on to their heirs. For my family, it has been a richly rewarding experience for the last quarter century to be ranchers and residents in this wonderful area.

In the next section, I will familiarize the reader with how we have managed our cattle operations. Words will be limited wherever photos will communicate more effectively as we walk through a typical year's activities.

Annual Ranch Activities

Winter Feeding

At the beginning of each new calendar year, the primary activity is simply to feed and look after the pregnant cows, keeping them in top condition for delivering their precious calves in a few months.

Photos this page by Rafael Routson

Calving

The gestation period for a cow is the same as for humans, nominally nine months, which allows ranchers to produce their calves during the same period each year (about two months). A healthy cow will normally drop a calf weighing 70 - 80 pounds. Twins are rare, but when they arrive, normally one calf is taken away and given to a cow that has lost her calf since the twin-calf cow usually can't produce sufficient milk for both.

It is necessary to check the cows every few hours during the calving season to assist as necessary any cows having trouble with delivery—although for 90%+ of the cows, the best thing to do is simply let nature take its course. First-calf heifers need more attention and more help.

Branding

The branding of our young calves is an event that takes place at our Centennial Ranch mid-April every year. We brand because the law and common sense dictates it be done. There are two methods of accomplishing this.

Many ranchers prefer to run the calves through a narrow chute, then into a "calf table" which is squeezed to constrain the animal before the table is tipped so the calf is horizontal. Then the various operations can be carried out such as vaccinations, de-horning and castration (if necessary), and then applying the brand with a hot iron before releasing the calf in an upright position.

Our method is the traditional "rope and drag" with a mounted cowboy roping the back legs of the calf, then dragging it to the branding area where the ground crew will throw the calf to the ground, remove the rope with one man securing the back legs, while another will hold the calf's head down with his leg on the neck. Then, all the operations can be performed and the calf released.

Most cattlemen are in agreement that the rope-and-drag method is less stressful on the calf.

In the century-old tradition of branding, neighbors and friends participate. When the work is done, all enjoy a great Bar-B-Que—and the occasional beer—courtesy of the hosting ranch. Here is what the branding operation looks like.

Chapter 13: Ranch Life

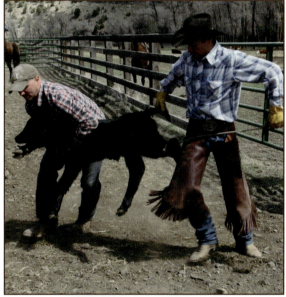

Photos by Natalie Heller

Volume 4: The Golden Years

Photos by Natalie Heller

Breeding

Some big outfits have gone to artificial insemination (AI) as an alternative to natural breeding. For us, there are more than a dozen reasons why AI doesn't make sense. Nature's way is the way to go.

We buy quality bulls of the traditional English breeds (either Angus or Hereford), keep them in excellent condition, then turn them out with the ladies on 15 May every year. The most recent result of pregnancies the year this is being written was 100%. Remarkable. I'm not sure if the credit goes to the randy bulls or the good-looking cows. No doubt a bit of both.

Summer in the High Country

In our mountainous country where the climate restricts hay production to the river valleys, the ranchers will move their livestock during the summer to graze on the rich alpine grass in the high country (above 8,000' in elevation). Some will utilize designated leases from government land, either the Forest Service or the Bureau of Land Management. However, our observation of government management of those leases encourages us to only lease from private owners.

We lease some 1,600 acres from the heirs of the Smith Brothers from whom we bought Centennial Ranch near Horsefly Peak. For more than two decades this has been a good arrangement for both parties.

About mid-June, once the snow is mostly gone from our lease and the grass has a good start, we will transport the cows and calves and the proper number of bulls from the ranch using 18-wheeler livestock haulers. The calves are simply too young to make the trek in a cattle drive as our lease is a good half-mile higher in elevation.

Sun spots on a cow inside the hauler.

Once the animals are off-loaded from the haulers, several of us on horseback will hold the herd in a fenced corner until the cows and their calves have paired up. Once released, they are on their own for the summer. We only check the cattle about once a week to spot any that need doctoring, set out salt and mineral blocks and inspect the perimeter fence in case our livestock could get out, or the neighbors in.

For the doctoring, we rely on what I think is a magic antibiotic, brown in color, that comes in a large bottle. When a cow gets a shot of this, it will cure all her ails, be they pinkeye, foot rot, or mild depression.

Photos this page by Natalie Heller

Haying

In the early summer with the cows on spring pasture, we focus on irrigating to optimize hay production. Once the ditch is free of snow, it is time to burn all the dead vegetation at the bottom and sides of the ditch. Care must be taken so as not to set the countryside alight.

The next task is to remove the sediment buildup in the ditch with a small excavator. When that is complete, water from the river will flow into the ditch once the headgate is opened.

The flood irrigation task lasts months, until the river level drops in the fall to below the headgate inlet. We get two cuttings of hay from our fields during the summer. For a long time we made small bales so we could handle them by hand for feeding with a team and hay wagon. When we lost one of our Belgians to eye cancer, we were forced to mechanize our haying and feeding operation.

When ready, we will cut the hay with a self-propelled swather and a few days later, will recover the dried hay from the windrows with a baler. This will produce for us the 1,000-pound round bales, which we store in a hayshed until they need to be retrieved for feeding in the winter.

Photos this page by Natalie Heller

Fall Gather

In late October, hopefully before any early snowstorm hits, it is time to bring the cows, with their calves alongside, down from the high country to the comfort and safety of the ranch in the valley. This is a two-day effort. First the gather (for whatever reason the local cowboys do not have the word "roundup" in their vocabulary), then the drive.

Normally the gather, from an 800-acre pasture, can be accomplished with 5-6 hours in the saddle for 4-5 riders. The livestock will be scattered over the pasture—in canyons, oak brush, aspens and near the ponds.

Once "gathered," the animals are held in a small wire-fenced corral to get a count. If any are missing, all hands scatter in different directions to find the strays. If the count is good, then the herd is moved about a mile to a 40-acre paddock with water and good grass to hold them for the drive the next morning.

Photos this page by Natalie Heller

Chapter 13: Ranch Life

Photos this page by Natalie Heller

> Our drive remains pure to tradition, three to five cowboys on good horses in the company of Jason's dogs.

Cattle Drive

Bringing our cattle down from the high country in a drive is a unique experience in the modern day. Only a few ranchers still do it, and frequently, those drives are contaminated with off-road ATVs, pickups, crazy dogs, amateur cowboys, et al.

Our drive remains pure to tradition, three to five cowboys on good horses in the company of Jason's dogs.

NATALIE HELLER

The path taken consists of narrow trails in ponderosa pine forests to vehicle tracks that serve those living off the grid, and then a few miles on a gravel county road before returning to jeep trails on BLM land. Finally, we drop off the high ridge at the western edge of the ranch in a steep dozer-cut into the side of the canyon wall to the ranch below.

The drive covers about 12 miles, and depending on conditions, will take six-plus hours. It is done rain or shine, and only delayed a day because of heavy snow.

For me, the cattle drive is as close to a religious experience as I ever experience.

Chapter 13: Ranch Life

Photos this page by Natalie Heller

Natalie Heller

Natalie Heller

Chapter 13: Ranch Life

Natalie Heller

Calf Sales

The final activity in our year-long ranch cycle is selling the calves born February to April. The calves we raise are among the best in the business. They are healthy, look good with excellent conformation and from their 70-80-pound birth weight, they will average some 600 to 700 pounds on a sale date in November.

After separating the heifers and steers, we will select about 10 heifers to be retained as replacements. We normally sell the remainder at the ranch, which eliminates the hassle and cost of transporting them to a sale barn then putting them up for auction in sorted lots of 10 to 20.

The quality of our calves are such that the buyers return each year with the calves weighed in lots of 10 on the ranch's antique Fairbank scales. A fair price to buyer and seller is then negotiated and the calves hauled in trailers to their new homes. By noon the calves are gone, the only cash crop of the ranch, and a new annual cycle begins.

It's a great life!

Photos by Natalie Heller

Commercial Photo Shoots

Location scouts and advertising agencies working for companies whose products require high-profile ads to attract customers have been pulled to Last Dollar and Centennial like iron filings on a tabletop are attracted to a strong magnet.

The unique photographic features at Last Dollar are the awesome backdrop of the Sneffels Range, the restoration of century-old log outbuildings and the log-and-stone barn, all without power poles and other modern-day landscape blemishes.

At Centennial, the attractions are the river, line cabin and timber-frame barn, as well as Dashwood House. We would generally welcome such ad shoots for it was a way to share the beauty of the ranches with which we live daily.

We worked closely with the producers and their crews, charging a modest fee with a request for some of their shots to have framed and displayed in our home. Actually, the only significant benefit to us was bragging rights.

The most frequent client was Marlboro for their print ads and billboards until they voluntarily ceased such advertising in the United States. However, they continued the ads for their international markets and their request for location shoots never ceased. Over the last quarter century, more Marlboro ads have been shot at Last Dollar than any other location in the United States. Marlboro has also come to Centennial numerous times—the last being just four months prior to this writing.

Budweiser brought some of their stable of Clydesdales to Last Dollar for video shoots that were shown to millions around the world, including a Super Bowl ad.

In addition, we have hosted shoots for cars and numerous requests to shoot ads for sports clothing. We'll show you a sample on the following pages.

Last Dollar Ranch
Tobacco clients: Marlboro/Copenhagen

"the Marlboro Man comes to Last Dollar Ranch"

Season's Greetings FROM MARLBORO COUNTRY

Volume 4: The Golden Years

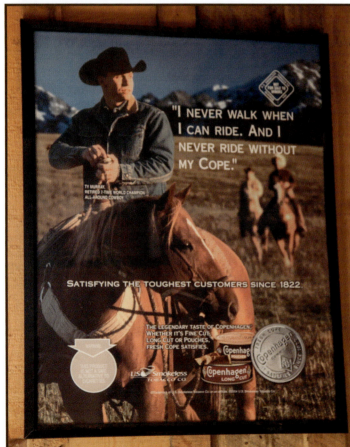

Chapter 14: Commercial Photo Shoots

205

Volume 4: The Golden Years

Beer clients: Budweiser, Coors, Anheiser Busch

Watch this complete video on youtube. Search Budweiser Clydesdale horses snowball fight.

Chapter 14: Commercial Photo Shoots

Watch this complete video on youtube. Search Budweiser Clydesdales commercial-Kiss.

207

Excerpts from Last Dollar Ranch *book.*

They found "Our Special Corner of Colorado."

CUT!!
It is time to do a commercial at The Ranch!
BUDWEISER
June 1980

Chapter 14: Commercial Photo Shoots

Excerpts from Last Dollar Ranch *book.*

COORS of Colorado comes to the mountain.

Westward Ho!....

Automotive clients: Pontiac, Ford, Honda

THE MONTANA WITH THE NEW-FOR-2002 VERSATRAK ALL-WHEEL-DRIVE SYSTEM (AVAILABLE) SHOWN IN GALAXY SILVER METALLIC OVER DARK CHARCOAL METALLIC.

Chapter 14: Commercial Photo Shoots

Montana: It's never been just another minivan. It's always been something more...with aggressive Pontiac styling, an adventurous attitude, a wagon-train full of practical features, and a truly rugged personality. And now with the addition of the available Versatrak all-wheel-drive system, Montana is even less like other minivans because it's now even more rugged...because excitement matters.

THE MOST RUGGED MINIVAN EVER

Consumer products clients: Marlboro Classics, Urban Outfitters, Minnesota Monthly, Territory Ahead, Marble Canyon

Chapter 14: Commercial Photo Shoots

213

Volume 4: The Golden Years

Chapter 14: Commercial Photo Shoots

Volume 4: The Golden Years

Centennial Ranch
Tobacco client: Marlboro

Chapter 14: Commercial Photo Shoots

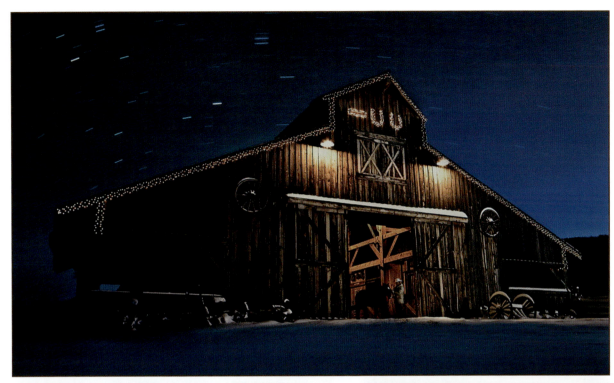

MARLBORO visits the ranch and they persuaded Rollen Smith to get his picture taken with them. From left is Rollen Smith, of the Smith Brothers Ranch, Marlboro man, Darrell Yates of Wyoming, and Jerry Dominick, of Salida, the other Marlboro man.

217

Volume 4: The Golden Years

Consumer products clients: Cabelas, Marlboro Classics, Abercrombie & Fitch, Territory Ahead, Urban Outfitters, Marble Canyon

Chapter 14: Commercial Photo Shoots

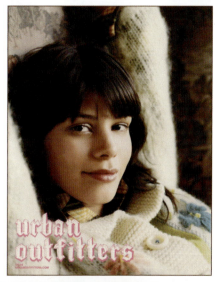

219

Volume 4: The Golden Years

Books, Magazines, Calendars and Catalogs

In addition to the photo shoots noted, the ranches have also been featured in a number of magazines and books including: *Architectural Digest, Cowboys & Indians, Country, Farm & Ranch, Colorado Homes, Log Home Living, Stables,* and *Ranches of Colorado.*

Chapter 14: Commercial Photo Shoots

221

Volume 4: The Golden Years

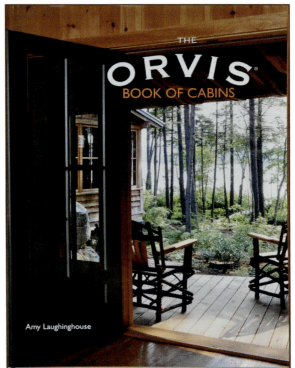

Chapter 14: Commercial Photo Shoots

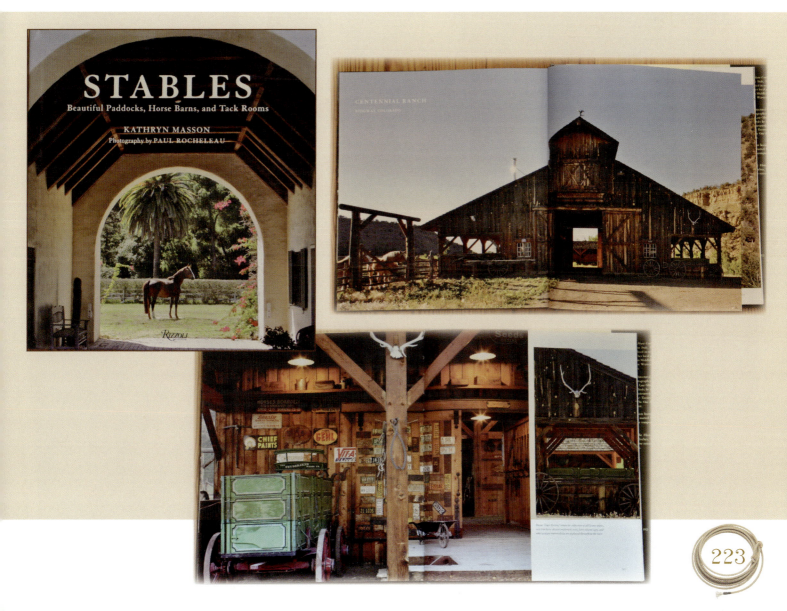

223

Volume 4: The Golden Years

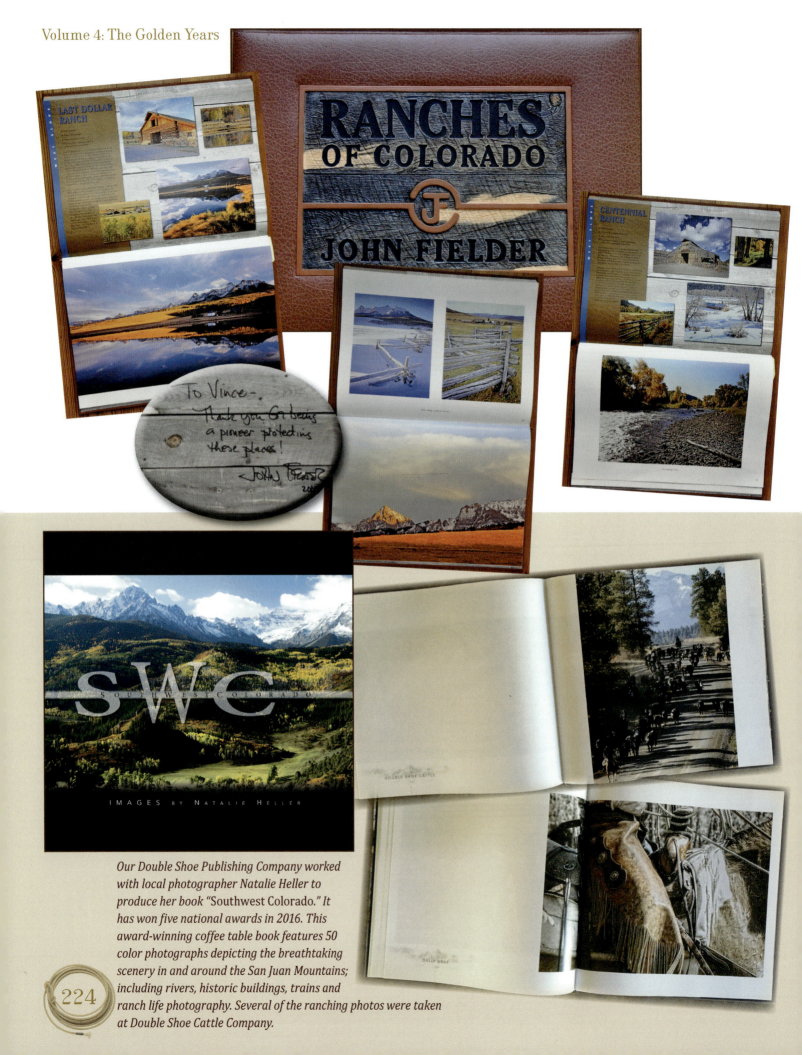

Our Double Shoe Publishing Company worked with local photographer Natalie Heller to produce her book "Southwest Colorado." It has won five national awards in 2016. This award-winning coffee table book features 50 color photographs depicting the breathtaking scenery in and around the San Juan Mountains; including rivers, historic buildings, trains and ranch life photography. Several of the ranching photos were taken at Double Shoe Cattle Company.

Chapter 15: Kids on the Ranch

Kids at the Ranch

NATALIE HELLER

Working cattle ranches are great places for kids to live or visit. There is nature, adventure, learning experiences, close contact with working people, farm animals and so much more. Maybe not the Magic Kingdom, but close!

Here, in no particular order, are some images of children enjoying our two ranches.

Volume 4: The Golden Years

Chapter 15: Kids on the Ranch

Volume 4: The Golden Years

Chapter 15: Kids on the Ranch

229

Volume 4: The Golden Years

Photos this page by Natalie Heller

Chapter 15: Kids on the Ranch

Volume 4: The Golden Years

NATALIE HELLER

Chapter 15: Kids on the Ranch

233

Volume 4: The Golden Years

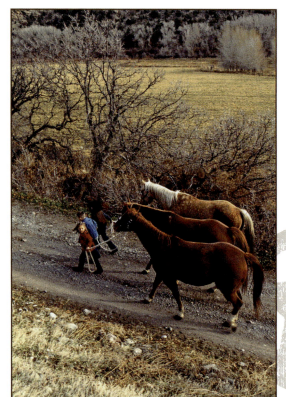

Natalie Heller

Chapter 15: Kids on the Ranch

Volume 4: The Golden Years

Chapter 15: Kids on the Ranch

Natalie Heller

Natalie Heller

Chapter 15: Kids on the Ranch

All Photos This Page by Natalie Heller

The Kontny Family 2013

Volume 4: The Golden Years

Double Shoe Publishing Company

As a way of sharing the ranches and capturing some of the history of the Old West, Joan and I started the Double Shoe Publishing Company. Our first efforts were to simply capture the history of our two ranches — the Last Dollar and the Centennial. Local historian Dona Freeman was instrumental in assembling the history and producing these three volumes; *Smith Ranch, Colona, Colorado; Last Dollar Ranch; Last Dollar Ranch 2nd Edition.*

Then, we sought to highlight the almost-lost art of blacksmithing. In the book *A Heritage in Iron*, we honored the skilled artisans who created the many pieces of functional ironwork on the ranches. My great niece, Rafael Routson, took on the challenge of producing this volume as well as the one that followed, *A Ranching Legacy*. Both of these books have received numerous accolades from the publishing industry.

Lastly, after enduring years of years of requests and cajoling from friends and family members, I decided it was time to capture some of my life's story on paper. Sisters Jeri and Jody Mattics along with my trusted administrative assistant, Barbara Parker, enthusiastically accepted the challenge of helping me move this project from my mind to paper to four completed volumes, the last of which you are holding in your hands.

Here is a little bit more information about each of the books that are still available in print.

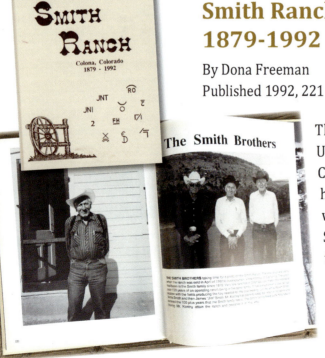

Smith Ranch, Colona, Colorado 1879-1992

By Dona Freeman
Published 1992, 221 pages (black and white)

This is a story of a pioneer family of the Uncompahgre Valley of Southwestern Colorado who came here in 1879. They homesteaded a ranch in the Colona area where James Nelson and Charlotte Eldridge Smith and their decendents would be on the "old home place" for 100 years. Vince and Joan Kontny renamed the ranch "Centennial" in recognition of the Smith's tenure when they purchased it in 1992.

Last Dollar Ranch

By Dona Freeman

Published 1993, 310 pages
(285 black and white; balance full color)

Capturing the history, heritage and hardships of the Last Dollar Ranch in Southwestern Colorado, this title is full of fascinating details about lives lived in the rugged San Juan Mountains as the area was settled. Beginning in 1872, the trials, tribulations and triumphs, along with an ample sprinkling of local folklore, are all included in this volume.

Last Dollar Ranch, Second Edition

By Dona Freeman

Published 2005, 360 pages
(285 black and white; balance full color)

We added an additional section to this book which contains color photos of the restoration of the ranch, and information about Double Shoe Cattle Company and the people who make it possible.

A Heritage in Iron

By Rafael Routson
Published 2004, 215 pages

This title is a tribute to the artists who designed and the blacksmiths that forged the exceptional ironwork on two historic Southwestern Colorado ranches. Praised by readers and judges alike, this book has earned three national book awards.

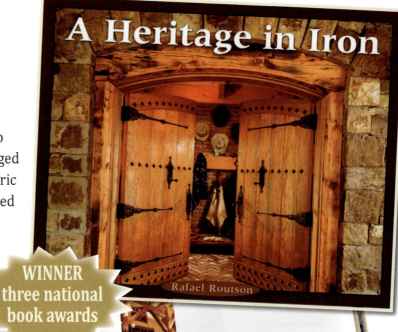

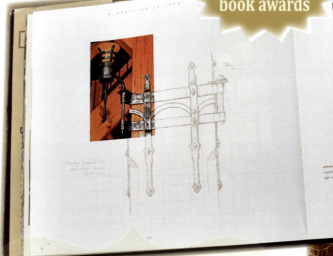

WINNER three national book awards

Judges Comments:
"Cover image invites readers in. Warm, illustrative of subject."

"Fascinating book from cover to cover. Exceptional blending of type and illustrations hold reader interest."

"Over-great shelf appeal."

"The photographs are excellent, as are all the graphics, and I particularly applaud the designer – beautiful, detailed work."

"I like that the ironwork information is set in a larger story of the various farms. The editor produced error-free, clear copy—sadly, this seems to be a rarity now!"

ForeWord Magazine
2005 Book of the Year Awards
Finalist – Architecture

Independent Publisher
2005 IPPY Awards
Finalist – Architecture

PubWest
Western Regional Book Design and Production Awards
First Place – Jacket/Cover Design
Runner-up – Art/Photography

Chapter 16: Double Shoe Publishing Company

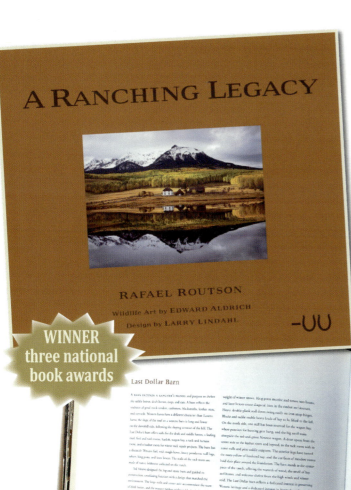

A Ranching Legacy

By Rafael Routson
Published 2005, 263 pages

This beautiful, full-color coffee-table book encompasses amazing photography and artwork along with eloquent text describing two historic working ranches in Southwestern Colorado that have been protected by conservation easements. This book has been recognized with three national book awards and effusive praise from readers.

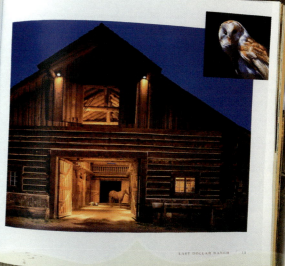

Writers Digest
2006 International Self-Published Book Awards
First Place – Non-fiction

ForeWord Magazine
2006 Book of the Year Awards
Finalist – Photography

Independent Book Publisher's Association
2006 Benjamin Franklin Awards
Finalist – Regional Titles

Judges Comments:
"Pretty incredible presentation. The prose is poetic without going too far from the subject. The family stories really take the reader into the world of ranching. The photos are gorgeous! And the small touches – draft horses, aspen carvings – really add to a feeling for 'the life.'"

"Best entry I received. Outstanding photography. Well-written and designed."

"Leather cover makes this book a must for display for anyone interested in the ranching lifestyle."

"Another fascinating book. I particularly like this one for its unusual entries – a collection of cast-iron implement seats, an actual bill of sale from the early 1900s. Also, the family feel of it."

243

The Life & Times of Vince Kontny, Volume 1: The Early Years

By Vince Kontny

Published 2010, 196 pages (full color)

The first in a four-volume series, this chronicle is filled with stories of life on the Great Plains, family values, travel and history; and how they inter-twined and influenced daily living. In addition to family history, the book explains day-to-day life in that period (~1937 – 1959). For example, Kontny tells of driving a tractor as a six-year-old boy, and of his family's involvement in the famous North Platte Canteen, which catered to servicemen on the troop trains stopping in North Platte, Nebraska, during World War II.

This book is attracting attention from award programs as well as other publications. An excerpt was featured in the April issue of *Country* magazine; another in the August/September issue of *Farm & Ranch Living* magazine.

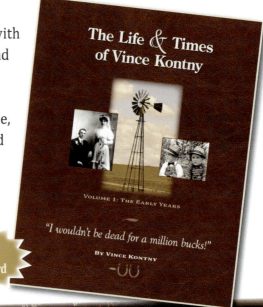

pg. 68–

"We definitely had heroes, but they were the real people we could observe working hard every day despite the task, the weather, or difficult economic challenges."

2011 National Indie Excellence Awards

Winner – Autobiography

Chapter 16: Double Shoe Publishing Company

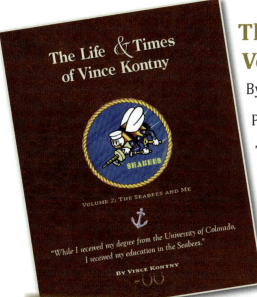

The Life & Times of Vince Kontny, Volume 2: The Seabees and Me

By Vince Kontny

Published 2011, 203 pages (full color)

The second in a four-volume series, this memoir covers the six tumultuous years the author served in the U.S. Navy Seabees in the Pacific and Southeast Asia during the 1960s. The story starts when a young farm boy from rural Colorado joins the Seabees and is sent to Rhode Island to attend Officer Candidate School. Part adventure story and part history, this book provides a glimpse of how the U.S. military trains its people, and how the Vietnam War escalated through a tragic series of well-intended, albeit misguided, decisions.

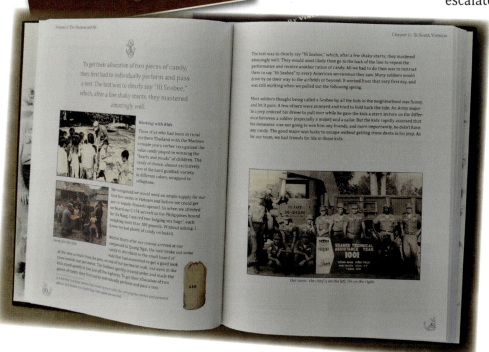

pg. 56–

"The last Marine to come off the ground was General Simpson. He was a great leader and inspiration. He remains to this day the most admired flag officer I met in my days with the Seabees."

The Life & Times of Vince Kontny, Volume 3: A Career in Construction

By Vince Kontny

Published 2013, 392 pages (full color)

The third in a four-volume series, this memoir covers the wide-ranging and adventurous career of its author in the global construction industry. The story begins when a Colorado farm boy hires on as a laborer to build a concrete grain elevator and follows him to railroad work in Alaska and into the Australian Outback.

After these early experiences in construction, the author records his life in the ranks of Fluor Corporation—an industry leader. When he retired as president and chief operating officer, Fluor was the largest engineering/construction company in the world. Readers will enjoy a vicarious journey as the author recounts the challenges and opportunities that presented themselves during construction projects on all seven continents.

Far from being a technical trade publication, this book offers real-life examples of how attitude and leadership can make all the difference between success and failure. Additionally, readers are offered a behind-the-scenes look at how large, public corporations can grow, stumble, right themselves and grow again based on decisions made at the top. Whether you're interested in construction, leadership or are a student of management, this book provides significant insight along with global adventure.

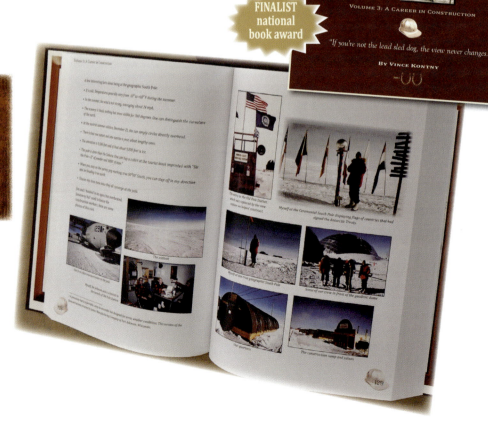

2014 Next Generation National Indie Excellence Awards

Finalist– Career Category

Chapter 16: Double Shoe Publishing Company

The Life & Times of Vince Kontny, Volume 4: The Golden Years

By Vince Kontny

Published 2016, 272 pages (full color)

The final volume in this four-part series covers the time and activities of the author's life as a rancher in Southwest Colorado. This book attempts to give the reader a feel for the place, people and history of these two ranches, and the western lifestyle along with the effort to preserve these for future generations.

pg. 15–

"I was as excited as I have ever been. The possibilities were endless, and just driving up the track to the homestead, my lifelong dream of a ranch with contented cattle grazing in the meadows, a log-and-stone barn for the horses in the shadow of towering rugged mountains with timber-covered slopes—seemingly close enough to touch—was visualized."

To order books, please visit www.doubleshoepublishing.com.